Living the Twelve Traditions in Today's World

Mel B. and
Michael Fitzpatrick

Living the Twelve Traditions in Today's World

Principles Before Personalities

Foreword by
William L. White

HAZELDEN®

Hazelden
Center City, Minnesota 55012
hazelden.org

Library of Congress Cataloging-in-Publication Data

B., Mel.
   Living the twelve traditions in today's world : principles before personalities / Mel B. and Michael Fitzpatrick.
      p. cm.
   Includes bibliographical references.
   ISBN 978-1-61649-196-3
1. Alcoholics--Rehabilitation. 2. Alcoholics Anonymous. 3. Twelve-step programs. 4. Group facilitation. I. Fitzpatrick, Michael, 1959- II. Title.
   HV5275.B23 2012
   616.86'106--dc23

                                        2012007665

Editor's note
The names, details, and circumstances may have been changed to protect the privacy of those mentioned in this publication.
   This publication is not intended as a substitute for the advice of health care professionals.
   Alcoholics Anonymous, AA, the Big Book, the *Grapevine, A.A. Grapevine,* and *GV* are registered trademarks of Alcoholics Anonymous World Services, Inc.
   The Twelve Steps and Twelve Traditions (long form) and brief excerpts from *Twelve Steps and Twelve Traditions, Alcoholics Anonymous,* and *A.A. Comes of Age* are reprinted with permission of Alcoholics Anonymous World Services, Inc. (AAWS). Permission to reprint brief excerpts from A.A. material does not mean that AAWS has reviewed or approved the contents of this publication, or that AAWS necessarily agrees with the views expressed herein. A.A. is a program of recovery from alcoholism *only*—use of its material in connection with programs and activities which are patterned after A.A., but which address other problems, or in any other non-A.A. context, does not imply otherwise.

21   4 5 6 7

Cover design by Percolator
Interior design and typesetting by David J. Farr, ImageSmythe

Legacy 12
Bringing AA and Twelve Step History Alive

Hazelden's *Legacy 12* publishing initiative enriches
people's recovery with dynamic multimedia works
that use rare original-source documents to bring
Alcoholic Anonymous and Twelve Step history alive.

Dedicated to Bill W., the author of the Traditions

Contents

Appendices

Foreword

For most Americans, Alcoholics Anonymous (AA) is synonymous with addiction peer recovery, also known as mutual aid. Few are aware of the dozens of alcoholic mutual aid societies that pre-date AA. These include early Native American recovery circles, the Washingtonians, recovery-focused fraternal temperance societies, Dashaway Association, Ollapod Club, Ribbon Reform Clubs, Drunkard's Club, Godwin Association, Business Men's Moderation Society, Keeley Leagues, Brotherhood of St. Luke, Jacoby Club, and the United Order of Ex-Boozers, to name a few of the more prominent. And, of course, adaptations of AA's Twelve Step model to other drug problems and secular and religious alternatives to AA have grown exponentially since the mid-twentieth century—the latter including groups such as Women for Sobriety, Rational Recovery, Secular Organization for Sobriety, Moderation Management, SMART Recovery, LifeRing Secular Recovery, Millati

Islami, Celebrate Recovery, and the Buddhist Recovery Network—again to name just a few.

Two questions arise from the history of recovery mutual aid: (1) "Why is AA the standard by which all contemporary mutual aid groups are evaluated?" and (2) "Why did AA survive and flourish when so many of its predecessors did not?" Clues to these questions must be unraveled within AA's growth and international dispersion, its continuing adaptation to other problems of living, its influence on addiction treatment, and its larger influence on American culture. But understanding AA's achievements still does not identify the source of AA's historical survival, spread, and continued vitality.

When I began my research in the 1970s on the history of addiction recovery mutual aid groups, I started with the assumption that this mysterious source would be found in the unique set of prescriptions within AA's Twelve Steps and the larger recovery community in which the Steps are nested. That assumption was challenged when I found elements of AA's Steps and evidence of the power of sober fellowship in pre-AA mutual aid groups. (Many of those predecessors had viable programs of sobriety but could not find a way to survive as organizations.) More than three decades later, I've concluded that what most distinguishes AA from its predecessors and from its many contemporary alternatives rests more with AA's Twelve Traditions than with its Twelve Steps. The Steps clearly contain ingredients for personal regeneration, but the Traditions provide the glue that holds together everything that is AA. Without the Traditions, AA may well have shared the fate of groups such as the Harlem Club of Former Alcoholic Degenerates — with future generations wondering if their past existence was fact or fiction.

Anyone who wants to understand the secret of AA's survival and success must become a student of AA's Traditions — a unique set of principles that shaped an organizational structure that even AA's closest early friends were convinced could not work. Students of the Traditions must go first to AA's own literature on the Traditions, but Mel B. and Michael Fitzpatrick offer important new perspectives in their book *Living the Twelve Traditions in Today's World*. Mel B. has a long history of contribution to the understanding of AA (e.g., *Ebby: The Man Who Sponsored Bill W., Walk in Dry Places, My Search for Bill W., New Wine: The Spiritual Roots of the Twelve Step Miracle*), and author Mike Fitzpatrick is building his own body of contributions on AA (*1000 Years of Sobriety* — with William Borchert) and Al-Anon (*We Recovered Too*).

Living the Twelve Traditions in Today's World achieves two things. First, it tells the story of AA's Traditions: the contexts and circumstances and the people and events in which each Tradition arose. Second, it reveals how the Traditions are interpreted and used as a tool of guidance and problem-solving within AA groups today. Both are achieved by letting past and present AA members speak in their own voices. These authentic messages are the greatest contribution of *Living the Twelve Traditions in Today's World*.

Those who want to explore the secrets to AA's survival and success will find the following pages essential and enjoyable reading.

William L. White
Author, *Slaying the Dragon: The History of Addiction Treatment and Recovery in America*

Guide to the
Audio CD

The nineteen-track CD included with this book offers highlights from archival recordings of AA's early leaders: passages from speeches, interviews, and other sources. Dozen of hours of recordings were excerpted and adapted for inclusion in the book *Living the Twelve Traditions in Today's World*. While the CD contains some of this audio, it does not parallel the book exactly and is not intended as a "listen-along" disc. Instead, it serves as a collection of personal accounts and reflections told in these visionaries' own words — stories that, together, capture the spirit of AA.

This icon indicates that an audio track of the transcript is available. The number on the icon indicates the track number.

Audio Tracks

Total running time: approx. 77 minutes

1. Alcoholics Anonymous cofounder Bill W. speaks in July 1950 at the First International Convention of AA in Cleveland, Ohio, expressing the "hope that every alcoholic who journeys will find a fellowship of Alcoholics Anonymous at his destination." (1:13)

2. Ollie L., a AA member from Dallas, shares Tradition One at the First International Convention of AA in Cleveland, July 1950. (2:32)

3. In July 1960, Bill W. tells attendees at the Third International Convention of AA in Long Beach, California, "You can take everything you got with you and our complete blessings. All except the name Alcoholics Anonymous." (2:12)

4. Bill W. tells about his job offer from Charlie Towns in a 1951 speech in Chicago. (4:06)

5. Ollie L. from Dallas goes on to discuss Tradition Two at the First International Convention of AA in Cleveland, July 1950. (2:13)

6. In a 1947 speech in Memphis, Tennessee, Bill W. tells the story of the alcoholic and drug-addicted doctor who started an AA group in Shelby, North Carolina. (5:43)

7. In a 1985 speech, Barry L. shares a personal story about answering phones at the AA clubhouse in Manhattan. (2:25)

17. Traditions Eleven and Twelve are presented by Kylie from Boston at the First International Convention of AA in Cleveland, July 1950. (11:35)

18. Bill W. summarizes the Twelve Traditions at the First International Convention of AA in Cleveland, July 1950. (4:34)

19. In July 1960, at the Third International Convention of AA in Long Beach, California, Bill W. tells why he turned down an honorary doctorate from Yale. (5:18)

Introduction

By 1945, Alcoholics Anonymous was becoming an exciting success story with a proven track record. Having started with just two men meeting in 1935, it had grown to nearly a thousand groups with an estimated 25,000 members. AA was getting considerable notice in the media and was becoming known as the place to go if one had a drinking problem. With its rapid growth, there were signs that its reach could become worldwide. Though AA had problems, a main focus of its founders was to ensure that AA's very success would not cause it to self-destruct from the shortcomings that had destroyed other promising movements. While AA would have critics and detractors, its survival really depended on its own members and their devotion to its core principles. The core principles would be a protection from strong but misguided personalities who could lead the fellowship astray.

It was also clear, by this time, that the fellowship could not accept burdensome rules and regulations. Nell Wing, Bill Wilson's longtime secretary, wrote about it in her book *Grateful to Have Been There*.

> Bill took the advice of Earl T., founder of the Chicago group, and codified this experience in the middle forties. He was able to synthesize it into a set of guidelines for the survival, unity, and effectiveness of the fellowship. Initially, he labeled them "Twelve Points to Assure Our Future." Later they were named the "Twelve Traditions." Had Bill tried to call them rules or regulations, they might never have been accepted.
>
> As it was, however, it was pretty tough trying to sell them to the groups. They weren't ready to listen, a condition that came as no surprise to Bill, I'm sure. As he often said, the groups were interested and eager to have him share his own story and AA beginnings, but not to listen to any more "discussion about those damned Traditions." So, again at the urging of Earl T. in 1949, Bill reduced them into a "short form" and they were accepted at the convention in 1950.[1]

Since then, these twelve points have served remarkably well as guidelines for the fellowship. While there have been anonymity breaks and other violations, nothing has occurred to damage AA as a whole or to discourage alcoholics seeking recovery.

The case can also be made that the Twelve Traditions, like the Twelve Steps, convey sound principles for living. If AA members understand and accept the Traditions, they can also receive positive benefits in the way they live their lives. Many AA members have incorporated the principles of these Traditions into their businesses and personal lives and family lives.

Bill W., in writing and winning acceptance of the Traditions, had already accumulated experience with the pitfalls that AA would face in its growth. Both Bill and cofounder Dr. Bob S. had been members of the Oxford Group, which supplied many of the principles that later became codified as the Twelve Steps. Though highly successful in the beginning, the group became embroiled in controversy when its founder and leader had an unfortunate 1936 newspaper interview that brought wide criticism and may have partly compromised the group's spiritual mission. This undoubtedly helped convince the early AA members to separate from the group. Bill later said that the Oxford Group had shown them what to do and what not to do.

Albert Einstein said, "We have to do the best we can. This is our sacred human responsibility."[2] A quick look back through civilization and human culture reveals that man has always wanted more property, prestige, and power. Albert Einstein's quote simply encourages one to do his or her best.

Western society—and with the spread of capitalism, Eastern and other previously noncompetitive societies as well—extols winning and "beating the other guy" as virtues. As far back as most of us can remember, we have been taught to compete, to be better than or beat out the other fellow. This includes every aspect of life: education, sports, dating, and careers. Once we have a job, we're supposed to be the best and are taught to strive to not be satisfied until we're the manager, boss, supervisor, and so on. Companies have spent enormous sums of money attempting to supply their work forces with motivational tools to assist them in the pursuit of excellence. For most people, this is a positive goal, but for many, this really means beating the competition, and when we don't, it often reflects on our self-worth. When we are trained to believe that our worth is tied to winning, then when we lose, as we all inevitably will, we look for ways to compensate for the negative feelings about our selves and our place in the world.

The alcoholic has many character defects and personality traits that seem to cause him or her to drink, at least in the early stages of alcoholism. Story after story of sober AA members discloses a similar tale — "Drinking made me feel like I fit in." "When I drank, I felt like I was six feet tall and handsome." "It made my insides feel like what I thought you looked like on the outside." "That emptiness left and I felt okay." The consistency of these messages clearly reflects that alcoholics have had a very difficult time coping with life, an important factor often being the competitive environment in which they were raised.

By the time the alcoholic finds the way to AA, he or she has "hit bottom." Now, *hitting bottom* means different things to different people, but for the alcoholic it seems fairly universal: "I can't go on living this way. Drinking no longer works, but I can't stop." The book *Alcoholics*

Anonymous describes it using phrases such as "pitiful and incomprehensible demoralization"[3] and "seemingly hopeless state of mind and body."[4] Some alcoholics have been shunned by society and locked away while others have lost their jobs, families, and self-respect. One AA member said, "I've yet to see somebody show up at his first AA meeting on the tail end of a winning streak."

Bill Wilson clearly recognized that the alcoholic had a terrible time living comfortably within society and that most alcoholics could never get or stay sober on their own. Perhaps that's one reason he decided to introduce the Twelve Traditions to the fellowship. Lois Wilson said that Bill had studied many societies and governments prior to the writing of the Traditions. One AA member recently stated that Bill W. had created a new government with his Traditions. Of course AA doesn't consider the Traditions to be a government, but nevertheless, Bill W. was able to create guidelines that have held AA together for more than seventy-five years, and one reason for that may be that alcoholics finally have a place where personality and winning is less important than principles and group unity.

The early framework for the Traditions can be traced back to the foreword for the first edition of the book *Alcoholics Anonymous* — although at the time these guidelines had not yet been enlarged upon.

We, of Alcoholics Anonymous, are more than one hundred men and women who have recovered from a seemingly hopeless state of mind and body. To show other alcoholics precisely how we have recovered *is the main purpose of this book. For them, we hope these pages will prove so convincing that no further authentication will be necessary. We think this account of our experiences will help everyone to better understand the alcoholic. Many do not comprehend that the alcoholic is a very sick person. And besides, we are sure that our way of living has its advantages for all.*

It is important that we remain anonymous because we are too few at present to handle the overwhelming number of personal appeals which may result from this publication. Being mostly business or professional folk, we could not well carry on our occupations in such an event. We would like it understood that our alcoholic work is an avocation.

When writing or speaking publicly about alcoholism, we urge each of our Fellowship to omit his personal name, designating himself instead as "a member of Alcoholics Anonymous."

Very earnestly we ask the press also, to observe this request, for otherwise we shall be greatly handicapped.

We are not an organization in the conventional sense of the word. There are no fees or dues whatsoever. The only requirement for membership is an honest desire to stop drinking. We are not allied with any particular faith, sect or denomination, nor do we oppose anyone. We simply wish to be helpful to those who are afflicted.

We shall be interested to hear from those who are getting results from this book, particularly from those who have commenced work with other alcoholics. We should like to be helpful to such cases.

Inquiry by scientific, medical, and religious societies will be welcomed.[5]

A quick look at the original foreword reveals several Traditions of AA had already begun to take shape. That may not immediately seem very significant, but one must consider that at the time it was written, AA had fewer than one hundred members and but a small handful of groups. History reveals that the Twelve Steps were a product of the experiences of the early members, and the Twelve Traditions were a result of the experiences of the early groups.

The First Tradition ("Our common welfare should come first; personal recovery depends upon A.A. unity")[6] sets the stage for the next eleven Traditions and each builds upon the necessity of group unity and humility. The fellowship of Alcoholics Anonymous today seems to be dealing with many of the same issues that the pioneering members faced; concerns about membership, anonymity breaks at the public level, power struggles, singleness of purpose, and disunity. Some members fear these issues will be the destruction of AA, while others seem to maintain an attitude of "This too shall pass."

In the following chapters, the authors will examine many of the issues facing the AA fellowship today and present some interpretations of the Traditions both from a historical point of view and from members' beliefs and experiences today. Mel B.—historian, author, and member of AA—will share some of his perspective from more than sixty years in the program, while coauthor Michael Fitzpatrick will provide historical data in the form of original transcriptions taken from early recordings of pioneering members. In addition, the authors will share insights gained from interviews with current members about the state of AA's affairs today and the importance and application of the Twelve Traditions. We hope that this will not only give readers a valuable and entertaining history lesson, much of it told by the people who made that history, but will also enrich the recovery programs of those who are members of AA and other Twelve Step groups that are guided by the Twelve Traditions.

1
Our Common Welfare

The year was 1950. Alcoholics Anonymous was just fifteen years old with a membership of less than 100,000. The year marked several major events in AA that have become some of the most historically significant in AA's seventy-six-year history.

From July 28 to 30, AA held its first International Convention in Cleveland, Ohio. It was there that AA's cofounder, Dr. Bob, gave his farewell address; he passed away less than three months later. It was also at that memorable convention that the current form of the Twelve Traditions was adopted by the AA fellowship.

Bill W. made the following remarks at one of the meetings:

1 Twelve years ago this fellowship commenced to prepare a book. The book we know today as *Alcoholics Anonymous*. And in the last pages of its text, the book expressed a hope. Yes, it was more than a hope, it told of a dream

that we then in this fellowship had. And we expressed our hope and our dream in these words: "Someday we hope that every alcoholic who journeys will find a fellowship of Alcoholics Anonymous at his destination." To some extent this is already true. Some of us are salesmen and go about [the country]. Little clusters of twos and threes and fives have sprung up in other communities through contact with our larger family. Those of us who travel drop in as often as we can. This practice enables us to lend a hand at the same time avoiding certain alluring distractions of the road, about which any traveling man can inform us. Such was our dream and it has been given to only a few to see an impossible dream come true, almost in its entirety.

One wonders what could be added to what we have already seen and felt and heard in these last two or three days? The song of this assembly is gratitude. And we rejoice in our world unity. Now it's spread into some thirty-four countries and reflected back on us here. We rejoice that AA is still simple and more deeply meaningful than ever. Yes, this is the time for gratitude, a time for rejoicing. It may be too a time of happy reminiscence when we can think back a little upon the days of our birth, our childhood, and our adolescence. It may be a time when we can think together once more about those principles we resolved yesterday which may bind us together in unity for so long as God shall need us.[1]

Though Bill W. would later assert that anonymity should be a key Tradition, the first two Traditions

Our Common Welfare

emphasize the need for unity and recognition that AA's leaders should be only trusted servants, with the group's ultimate authority being a loving God as expressed through the group conscience.

A careful look at Tradition One shows that humility, through the deflation of personal power, false pride, and ego, will create the atmosphere required for the individual to recover. Twelve years after the Big Book was published, Bill elaborated on Step One; he indicated that once the alcoholic was able to fully admit that he or she was personally powerless, this declaration would eventually become the foundation upon which a full, sober, and happy life could be built.

The First Tradition creates a similar foundation, which guarantees that both the group and the individual can enjoy the same successful outcome.

When the Traditions were adopted and became a permanent part of AA at the Cleveland Convention in 1950, the convention committee selected six members from around the country to each speak on two Traditions. The first speaker was Ollie L. of Dallas, Texas.

2   Good evening, everybody. First I'll read the First Tradition: "Our common welfare should come first; personal recovery depends upon A.A. unity." I couldn't help but think just a second ago when I was going through a little moment of silent meditation, how different it was maybe four and a half years ago when I first came into AA — how different my little meditation was just that second ago. How I offered up a little quickie that this convention would be

good for everybody. That everybody would take home
with them the message that was intended for them to get
....And believe me, I can't help but feel like that might be
a weakness of maybe all of us. We did send up prayers of
all descriptions, most of them rather hollow, but maybe
we asked for a little bit more just for ourselves. The AA
Tradition as I understand number one is that Alcoholics
Anonymous, beyond all question of a doubt, must be
number one. Because without it, you and I certainly
wouldn't be here and certainly not in attendance at this
fine convention. We're only a part. We must forget our
big "I." We must forget everything but that AA must be
given a green light. And AA must be assisted. And we
must be, as I see it, a little bit jealous of what Alcoholics
Anonymous and what Alcoholics Anonymous as a group,
each of our groups, mean to us as a whole. We must forever [keep] it simple. We must keep it clean and unorga-
nized, and fair to every member.[2]

The general feeling of unity we have in AA today is
remarkable, especially since the membership is made
up of people who acknowledge false pride and resent-
ment as major personal problems. Right from the beginning, the AA pioneers envisioned in the Big Book that
"every alcoholic who journeys will find a Fellowship of
Alcoholics Anonymous at his destination."[3] This has
been true for decades, and it's now possible to find a
welcoming AA group throughout much of the world.
There's also unspoken agreement that the members
must get along with one another or alcoholics will die

without finding recovery. The First Tradition ensures this by simply stating "Our common welfare should come first; personal recovery depends upon A.A. unity."[4]

This same Tradition evens the playing field, making it certain that all members, regardless of their background and social standing outside of AA, have the exact same membership privileges — no bosses and no human authorities. Although many AA groups and members recognize and celebrate various lengths of continuous sobriety, that demonstration is to acknowledge that the program has successfully worked for those individuals. All members are exactly the same; consequently the newest member is equally as important to the group as the one who has been there the longest.

Each AA member represents one link in the chain of unity that holds the organization together. One member describes it this way: "If we took all the AA members and had them join hands, then had an aerial view, we would see everyone linked together. There would be no way to tell anything more about each individual other than that he or she is another link in the chain."

One might find personal fulfillment and understanding in seeing the AA movement as a ship with many passengers. While the officers and crew are responsible for the ship, every person on board has an interest in keeping the vessel afloat and ensuring that it reaches its destination. When joining AA, each member boarded a vessel that could take him or her safely through the many seas of life, with storms included. The attitude of sticking together or dying separately is a quiet theme.

But how is unity established and maintained? And since AA currently has about two million members, how can individual efforts be significant in preserving unity and the common welfare? For one answer, we can look at how the other Traditions naturally follow and support the First Tradition.

The goal of focusing on AA unity by excluding other controversial issues covered in Tradition Ten (regarding AA not having opinions on outside issues) has its critics from outsiders who admire AA's popularity and would like to enlist its support for other causes. Many years ago, for example, a political issue in one midwestern state arose over a proposal to put the recently formed state board of alcoholism into the state's health department. There were sound arguments for and against the proposal, but some AA members believed that AA members should oppose the proposal publicly because its adoption could reduce the effectiveness of the alcoholism board. Even acknowledging that AA groups should not engage in public political issues, they argued that this issue was so important it required an exception to tradition. But there was no opposition to the proposal in AA's name, and the state merged its alcoholism unit into the health department, with no apparent serious consequences.

During that same time period, civil rights became one of the most explosive issues on the national scene. Some AA groups in certain parts of the country excluded minorities in line with current customs of their region. Bill W., who strongly believed in equal treatment for everybody, must have been tempted to address this issue in his articles for the general AA membership. He made no such statements, but by personal example he made it clear that the AA program and membership should be available to everybody. In the early 1940s, when his New York group voted to not accept two black alcoholics he had invited to the meeting, he stepped away from a bitter fight over the matter. Instead he asked the group to take a second vote on whether blacks should be offered the AA program just like the other folks. When they voted in the affirmative, he persuaded the group to admit the blacks as "observers" to learn how the program works. In a short time, the group was fully integrated with no brawling or bloodshed.

While speaking at AA's Third International Convention held in Long Beach, California, in July of 1960, Bill W. had this to say about AA's unity:

> 3 We are division-proof because we can safely invite division. We don't, like this country once did, have to fight a civil war to stay united. We fight lots of civil wars, to be sure, but not to be united. What can we do? A fellow says, "I don't like my group." We say, "For heaven sakes, start another one."
>
> Now it is a curious fact about AA, that the individual has had practically all the grief there is, his group or certainly the early groups, had nearly every trouble known to the mind of man...and yet never in the whole history of this society has a great issue cut across us to divide us. And lest we be caught unaware, let us ask ourselves

what we ought to do if that threatens. Our first reaction would say, "My God, we must hold this thing together. They must not go." But why shouldn't we take the same attitude that we do every day on a smaller scale, and say, "Good friends, we have no pride of membership. We have no property to quarrel about. We have no authority to defend. If you think you can do better under other auspices, by all means go and try. You can take everything you got with you and our complete blessings. All except the name Alcoholics Anonymous. We'd kind of like to hang on to that one. And when you arrive where you're going under new ideas or under new auspices and you do better and you grow faster in numbers and in recovery and in maturity and in freedom under God, Alcoholics Anonymous is going to take some lessons from you people. But if it so turns out that your death rate mounts and your discontent mounts and the old obsession is back in full force, and you haven't any more choices, you'll just be so damned glad to come back to Alcoholics Anonymous that it's nobody's business."

So, here is the whole world, which fears for fission and division and we have nothing to fear because this is an inherent advantage, let me emphasize again, not a virtue. It's a kind of singular gift of God to us; that the fears of the world outside, in a greater part, need not be ours at all.

Now, however, there comes this question of prudence. And prudence is a kind of a sound halfway point, somewhere between fear and recklessness. The "middle-road" I think the greats used to call it. So a lot of these Traditions deal not with fear, they deal with prudence and prudence means anticipation. And it means those ideas and attitudes that can avoid temptation.[5]

As the AA fellowship prepares to celebrate its next measurable milestone, the 100th anniversary of the founding which will take place in June 2035, members will surely look back and appreciate the foresight of Bill W. and the other pioneers. For these individuals recognized that AA's survival could only come through collective group unity and by placing the common welfare of all the members first, above everything else. For without this, surely there would be no recovery.

2

One Ultimate
Authority

Learning about AA for the first time, some people are surprised that AA has none of the trappings of authority that are typical of other societies and movements. There is no one person or group that can order AA members around. Even the General Service Conference (GSC), established in the early 1950s, has only the power to make suggestions and issue "advisory" actions.

It must have been divine guidance that led Bill W. to suggest that an AA group should have but one ultimate authority: "For our group purpose there is but one ultimate authority — a loving God as He may express Himself in our group conscience. Our leaders are but trusted servants; they do not govern."[1] This concept of one ultimate authority is still widely accepted in AA, so much so that the planners of the 2015 International Convention extracted it from the Second Tradition as the convention's theme.

In explaining how this concept works in a 1951 speech given in Chicago, Bill W. talked about a time in AA's very early days when he was offered a position that would have given him the opportunity to combine his AA activity with a money-making venture. It came when he was flat broke, and at first he thought it didn't seem to compromise his AA work. But his allies in the program were opposed to it. He accepted this as God speaking through the group conscience and passed up the offer. Bill felt that his experience so well illustrated the group conscience that he shared the story often when speaking about how the Traditions developed.

Here's an excerpt from that speech:

4 We were deeply convinced, for example, that the survival of the whole was more important than the survival of any individual or group of individuals; that this is a thing far bigger than any of us. We began to suspect that once a mass of alcoholics were adhering even halfway to the Twelve Steps that God could speak in their group conscience. And up out of that group conscience could come a wisdom greater than that of any inspired leadership.

And I used to think that I was one of these inspired leaders, but boy I got un-horsed good. Let me tell you a story about the kind of temptations we used to have. One time when things were awful tough, drunks around New York were getting well; lots of them got pretty good jobs. It was just before Lois and I got evicted from the house. I was up at Towns Hospital one day. Old Charlie who'd lent us money on the book that was about to go bust

[*Note:* Bill is referring to the early challenges publishing the first edition of *Alcoholics Anonymous*] called me in his office and he said, "Look Bill," he said, "you're passing all these people up over your head. They're all getting good jobs; they're getting back to work. You're spending all the time getting these people well, but you're starving to death. That isn't right." He said, "Why don't you come up here and take an office in my place; let me give you a drawing account?" Back here in the 1920s this place used to earn several thousand dollars a month.

He said, "I'm no great man of the spirit but," he said, "I can see this thing is going to work. You're going to fill Madison Square Garden someday with these drunks."

"Well," I said, "That's a little optimistic. You don't know 'em as well as I do."

But anyhow, said he, "Why don't you come in here. I'll give you a third interest in the place. Actually, you had this funny experience of yours here. Dr. Silkworth helped you out. That could be advertised in a perfectly ethical way."

Well you know it sounded awfully good to me, I don't mind saying. And then began that process of rationalization to which we drunks are so very subject. I began to think of Lois still in the department store. And then I got a dandy rationalization right out of the Bible, the good book itself. On the way home, one of those illuminated thoughts came into my mind, you know. And it said to me, "The laborer is worthy of his hire." And so I get home and Lois is cooking the supper and I say, "Honey, we're going to eat. And no fooling, we're going to work up at Charlie Towns." And we thought how nice it would be to be able to pay our bills. And there was a little meeting in the front parlor that evening. I started to enthusiastically tell my fellow alcoholics of this bright new opportunity. And rather challengingly I asked them, some of whom were making good livings, "Isn't the laborer worthy of his hire?"

I could tell by the look in their eyes. And finally, rather timidly one of them said, "Bill, don't you realize that would create a professional class? Don't you realize that would marry us to that particular hospital? Oh sure, it's ethical in the book of ethics. But Bill, it isn't good enough for us. Aren't you the very man who has so often told us, 'Sometimes the good is the enemy of the best'? No, Bill, that isn't good enough for us. You can't do that to us." So spoke the wisdom of the group. So spoke the group conscience to me. And for the first time I realized that this movement, this society had begun to speak to me and teach me and I knew that when they spoke truly, I must obey. And I did.[2]

Bill realized the importance of self-sacrifice and of giving up personal demands in favor of the group. Seemingly, at every opportunity, he would point the finger of guilt or blame at himself in lieu of possibly creating conflict or dissension among members. His willingness to lead by example and serve others was constantly demonstrated by his eagerness to adhere to the AA Traditions. His ability to hold fast to this particular Tradition probably saved AA from an early destruction.

Many of the early groups' founders and pioneering members resisted the idea of the group conscience, believing this was an attempt by the New York office to strip them of their self-appointed positions and remove them from power. These groups were thriving, and many of them had rules and regulations that at that time were enforceable by the group leaders. Some of these groups used extreme measures to keep out undesirables.

In one case, a woman wanting to attend the AA meeting in Los Angeles back in 1941 received a letter from the local AA group. This letter has been circulated for years and is being included here to show that before the Traditions were in place many members and groups were making decisions that could have led to AA's demise.

ALCOHOLICS ANONYMOUS
Post Office Box 607
Hollywood Station
Hollywood, California

December Fifth 1941

Irma L.
Los Angeles, California

Dear Mrs. L.:
At a meeting of the Executive Committee of the Los Angeles Group of Alcoholics Anonymous, held Dec. 4th, 1941, it was decided that your attendance at group meetings was no longer

*desired until certain explanations and plans
for the future were made to the satisfaction
of this committee. This action has been taken
for reasons which should be most apparent to
yourself. It was decided that, should you so
desire, you may appear before members of this
committee and state your attitude. This
opportunity will be afforded you between now
and December 15th, 1941. You may communicate
with us at the above address by that date.*

*In case you do not wish to appear, we shall
consider the matter closed and that your
membership is terminated.*

Alcoholics Anonymous, Los Angeles Group [3]

This example of a group action may seem extreme
to some today, but it was this type of experience that led
to the formation of the Traditions. And again, a lesson
was learned from the Oxford Group, which practiced
"team" guidance for individuals. Bill W. was even told
by some group members that they had been guided to
tell him he should stop working with alcoholics. While
he continued to believe in divine guidance, he did not
accept that this was anything more than the opinions of
a few people.

A second concept in this Tradition is that AA's leaders "are but trusted servants; they do not govern." If any
AA member has trouble accepting leadership, this idea

should put his or her fears to rest. The AA group may be one of the best places to learn about leadership. As a trusted servant, one can only suggest and negotiate to get things done. It can be a wonderful surprise to learn that this works better, at times, than a command system. An AA member whose professional work includes barking out orders to subordinates can actually discover another approach in the AA setting. Be a trusted servant in AA and you might also be a better coworker and boss!

Bill W. knew AA members could have a tendency to want to control the group. He realized that even though it was helpful to have an elder member step up and organize things when the group was first beginning, in time it would be harmful to both the member and the group if he or she remained in that role and assumed a position of authority. In the book *Alcoholics Anonymous Comes of Age,* he wrote about it.

> *Harder still to accept was the now proven fact that the conscience of the group, when properly informed of the facts and issues and principles involved, was often wiser than any leader, self-appointed or not. We slowly realized that the old-timer frequently was faulty in judgment. Because of his position of assumed authority, he was too often influenced by personal prejudices and interests. With all his experience and good works, there was still nothing infallible about him at all.*
>
> *Does this mean that as old-timers our usefulness is over? No. Once we old-timers have surrendered to the Group Conscience we are pleasantly surprised to find that*

the groups, when in deep difficulty, will again turn to us for the kind of guidance that only our longer experience can give.[4]

Bill often referred to an old-timer who resisted the group conscience and attempted to force his will upon the group as a "bleeding deacon." However, when one of these old-timers conformed to the group conscience, he would be that group's elder statesman.

When this Second Tradition was introduced to the membership at the Cleveland Convention, Ollie L. shared about it.

5   Number two — for our group purpose there is but one ultimate authority — a loving God as He may express Himself in our group conscience. Our leaders are but trusted servants; they do not govern. We all know that there are no "big shots" in AA. We all know that each of us, as a member of AA, understands AA in his own way. We come to Cleveland and I have seen a lot of people that I admire with their long years of sobriety. I do like to see their grace and their ease and the manner in which they conduct themselves. And if I don't watch myself I will become maybe a little bit jealous of a lot of them. That is not the AA way. Rather, I'll respect them, and I'm glad to see such fine guys and girls that came in ahead of me and paved the way for this thing that I know is my salvation today. Number One: Alcoholics Anonymous and then I'll put myself in there. I'll get what I can out of the program, always keeping in mind that if I don't put Alcoholics

Anonymous first, that if l do not listen and heed well to those . . . [who] have made a success, of personal success, out of the way in which they handle the AA program, then l have erred someplace. I want Alcoholics Anonymous to always be number one in my life. And a long time ago it wasn't. Thank you very much.[5]

The spirit of rotating service positions at the group level also came out of these experiences. Active groups create rotating service positions, such as group secretary, general service representative, treasurer, chairperson, coffee maker, door greeters, and a host of others positions depending on the size of the group. These service opportunities become very effective tools in helping the members to learn responsibility and commitment. Many longtime members reflect back on their early sobriety with statements such as, "I stayed sober because I had to make the coffee," "I had to set up chairs, so I never missed a meeting," "I felt like I belonged because people were counting on me." The list goes on.

Today's AA is much the same. When new members feel as though they are a part of a group or others are counting on them, many rise to the occasion and sobriety seems to follow. It's said over and over, "If you want to stay sober, get a service position." These are the group leaders; they do not govern, they only serve. One longtime member said, "The greatest you can ever be in AA is a servant to others — it's that spirit of service in action that produces emotional sobriety."[6]

3
No Barriers
to Entry

Back in 1941, a kindly judge in Pontiac, Michigan, gave an alcoholic named Chauncey C. the opportunity to attend AA meetings rather than go to jail for a recent drinking offense. At first Chauncey, who had lived on the street and considered himself a blue-collar worker, wondered if he belonged because some of the members he met were doctors and lawyers and he felt outclassed. But it turned out in a wonderful way, and Chauncey went on to chalk up more than sixty-five years of sobriety before he passed away as a much-loved AA member and a friend to all.

Chauncey quickly discovered the concept of the Third Tradition before it had even been written: that a desire to stop drinking is the only requirement for AA membership. Like AA members before and after, he learned that AA should have no entry barriers related to race, age, occupation, gender, class, educational level, or social standing. Any alcoholic can join simply by expressing a desire to quit drinking. Even in 1941, the AA group Chauncey found in the nearby upscale community of Birmingham, Michigan, was open to anybody who wanted to join.

While this Tradition is generally accepted today, some early AA groups did attempt to impose certain rules for admission to AA. But these efforts were soon dropped when it became clear that they had little relevance to recovery. Just as alcoholism strikes without respect to persons, it is equally true that recovery comes about in the same way. This is consistent with AA's acceptance that alcoholism is an illness that occurs randomly throughout the general population.

There are now special groups within AA, with meetings designated specifically for people according to their gender, sexual orientation, cultural background, professional affiliation, and so on. While any alcoholics with a desire to stop drinking would be welcomed to any of these meetings, if they don't belong to the special population that the group was formed to serve, they are generally referred to a more traditional group. AA World Services doesn't officially condone this practice, but it also recognizes each group's autonomy to address its specific needs. The first known exclusive meeting for men began in Cleveland, Ohio, in 1941 under the name Crawford Men's Group. The name was changed to Doan Men's Stag, and in March 1945 it was changed to Doan Men's Group. This meeting is still held every Wednesday night at 8:00.

But most AA meetings are open to all who identify themselves as alcoholics. This is in keeping with the Third Tradition and has been largely successful.

There is a surprising benefit to this Tradition that few recognized in the beginning—that of forming close friendships with people one never would have met before joining AA. The AA fellowship includes people who may have nothing in common, except their desire to overcome alcoholism. The Big Book puts it this way:

> *We are people who normally would not mix. But there exists among us a fellowship, a friendliness, and an understanding which is indescribably wonderful. We are like the passengers of a great liner the moment after rescue from shipwreck when camaraderie, joyousness and democracy pervade the vessel from steerage to Captain's table. Unlike the feelings of the ship's passengers, however, our joy in escape from disaster does not subside as we go our individual ways. The feeling of having shared in a common peril is one element in the powerful cement which binds us.*[1]

When Bill W. talked about the Third Tradition, he never wavered from the original intention made in the first edition of the Big Book: that the only requirement for membership was a desire to stop drinking. The goal of this Tradition has always been for AA to be all-inclusive and never exclusive. Providing, of course, that would-be members simply have a drinking history and consider themselves to be alcoholics. Without that important qualification, the identity and commonality between members would be diminished, as would the effectiveness of the program.

Certainly the pioneering members took into consideration problems other than alcohol when agreeing upon this very important Tradition. In today's AA, it is a novelty to have a new member come to a meeting who hasn't also had difficulty with other drugs. The AA Tradition is very clear regarding this sometimes sensitive issue. Does this person have a drinking history? And a desire to stop drinking?

In 1947, in one of Bill W.'s earliest recorded talks, he told the following story, which seems to address this issue very well. Bill enjoyed telling stories and for this reason the entire story is shared here.

6   Speaking of Southern hospitality, reminds me of one of the greatest stories ever to come out of Alcoholics Anonymous. And I saw the beginning of that story while enjoying the hospitality of an AA over in Shelby, North Carolina.

It was some six years ago; we had made our start; we were getting on firmer ground here and there. But nothing was too certain, and one day our central office in New York — which is merely a service center where we receive inquiries and one thing and another — one day that office received a letter from a man who was an inmate of the Lexington place for drug addicts. And he went on to tell us in the letter how he had been a physician, had got onto alcohol, and then onto morphine, and that while there in the asylum someone had written him about AA. And he had been reading this AA book of ours, which is our book of experience. And he said, "Of course, I used to be an alcoholic, but now I'm an addict of some twelve years' standing, and you know how hopeless that is. But I do see hope for me in this philosophy of yours, and when I get out of here I'm certainly going to try it."

Well, subsequently our office struck up correspondence with him, as he'd returned home to that little southern hamlet. He told us in his quiet way of his various difficulties he'd had, but never in any complaining sense. And the girls in the office would write him occasional letters of encouragement, and little by little he began to describe the formation of an AA group in Shelby — by the way one of the earliest groups that we have formed in the mail, just through mail contact.

Well, it was a great thrill to all of us in the office. Meanwhile, other southern centers had started — Atlanta, Jacksonville. In larger places the groups had become larger. And a demand had arisen that I get down among the Southerners and pay my respects and see if I couldn't peddle a little of the older AA experience down there.

Well, you see, AA had begun to look like a success at that time, and as everyone knows, success is a heady wine, and I fear that I was a little bit on the "big shot" side and I spent some little time debating with the folks in the office whether I really would stop off at Shelby. I mean, you know that chap there was a nice chap and he'd done a nice job, but I should get where I could get to a lot of people and after some debating with myself I finally grudgingly conceded that I would stop off there at Shelby.

Well, I alighted from the train and I saw three men approaching me down the platform. Two of them I spotted as "souses" right off the bat, you couldn't mistake it — they were sober, understand. The third one, well I wondered who he was. And as he drew near, I saw some lines in his face I didn't quite place . . . As he drew nearer, I saw that his lips were marked and I learned later, in the agony of his dope hangovers he had chewed them.

And he turned out to be a delightful, soft-spoken little man who I shall call Dr. Tom. Well, we got in the car and drove from Kings Mountain over to Shelby and we were set down at the door of one of your delightful ancestral homes. And we went inside and there I met Tom's mother and a wife of two years and a child, and you could feel the atmosphere of that home. The meal came and went and . . . I found that Tom was rather reluctant to talk about what he had done in Shelby, so there wasn't much AA "shop talk" at the table (practically unheard of elsewhere). And I wondered myself if dope had a humbling effect — if so, I think that some of us alcoholics should have taken more of it.

At any rate, presently meeting time came, and we got down there. And the meeting place was right under the hotel — was right next to the barber shop — very public. I said, "Well now, for a small town that's really going some." Yes, and even over the door, here were two letters — AA. I got in and saw the usual gay crowd and then the meeting started.

Well, now up in New York — incidentally, I'm not from New York so I say what I'm going to say with impunity

(I'm a Vermonter, and therefore one of the damnedest of Yankees) — there is a saying that New York is not in America, our group there is very cosmopolitan and we have vast numbers of what you might call "stumble bums." We have a great many sophisticates of very wise people there, or at least we used to until AA tamed them down.

In those days we used to rather have to pussy-foot in New York on the subject of God, lest we scare away some of the intellectuals. So when I got to Shelby and there was a great long invocation and a choir girl got up and sang a hymn — well it was reminiscent of my youth in Vermont. But I said to myself, "Well, now, the New Yorkers wouldn't call this AA."

Then they called upon me to talk and I talked too long — by the way, shut me off any time you get tired tonight. I have that habit. Then I believe there was another long prayer and the meeting was over. I began to notice with amazement that there were an awful lot of AAs there, I mean twenty, thirty of them in this small place, and they told me there was an equal out in the defense industry and I was wonderfully and favorably stirred by the whole thing. The crux of my story turned around with what happened the next morning.

I was to leave on an early train and somebody called up from the lobby and said, "Do you mind, Bill? I'd like to drop up and tell you a few things about Dr. Tom." The man came up and he said, "I've got some things you should know. Speaking of myself, I once organized a string of banks in these Southern states. I was on a high road to success. I was cut down by alcohol and then I was cut down by morphine and I have been in the asylum with Dr. Tom. And when he heard that I was leaving for one of my many trips there, he asked me to come here. And I've stayed here to work with him. And I have been all right myself now a year, and he about three." And he said, "You know, I'm very gladly sweeping out the Masonic Temple, just so I can have time to help my friend Dr. Tom. But enough about me; let me tell you about Dr. Tom."

Do you realize when that man came back here to this little town — can you possibly comprehend what the stigma was upon him? The stigma of both alcohol and morphine; he had dishonored his profession of medicine and his highly placed family in this community. People were so afraid; they hardly spoke to him on the street. And he said, "I'm sorry to say that even the drunks of Shelby were snobbish, saying that they weren't going to be sobered up by no damned drug addict." Little by little he began to work, and little by little he began to succeed and the group grew.

"Well," said this man, "you've been at Tom's home, you have seen that happy mother of his, you've seen the new wife and you've seen the new baby, but you still don't know the whole story. Tom now has been made the head of our local hospital. He probably has the largest medical practice in the county today, all this accomplished in three years from a start way behind the line. And we've a yearly custom in this town in which all the citizens take a vote on which one of them has been the most useful individual to the community in the year past. Last spring Dr. Tom was."

When the man finished his recital, l said to myself, "So you were the man, Bill Wilson, who was too important to go to Shelby."[2]

One can easily see that Bill was grateful for Tom's sobriety and the contributions he has made to the community of Shelby, both within AA and in the public. Of course, if Alcoholics Anonymous had put too many restrictions on Tradition Three, Dr. Tom most certainly wouldn't have qualified.

General society has also gone through major changes since AA was founded. In 1985, a talk was given by Barry L., a relatively early gay member who would later author *Living Sober*.

> 1968 was the last time he [Bill W.] was able to address the General Service Conference before he died. Bill made a talk on all the Traditions and l was there because it was my job to write the conference report; not because l was a member of the conference, [l was] not a voting member — l wrote the conference reports for many years. Listening to Bill talk on the Traditions was old hat; l'd heard it many times and l didn't pay attention to it.
>
> But recently a dear friend of ours in Brooklyn called me and told me that he had found something quite remarkable that Bill said in 1968 and that l ought to hear this tape. . . . He had emphysema very badly, and it was not easy for him to talk and you could tell on the tape. Here is what he said. *[Plays recording of Bill W.]*

"At about year two of the Akron group a poor devil came to Dr. Bob in a grievous state. He could qualify as an alcoholic, all right; and then he said, 'Dr. Bob, I've got a real problem to pose to you. I don't know if I could join AA because I'm a sex deviate.'

Well, that had to go out to the group conscience. You know up to then it was supposed that any society could say who was going to join it. And pretty soon the group conscience began to seize and boil, and it boiled over. And under no circumstances could we have such a peril and such a disgrace among us, said a great many. And you know right then our destiny hung on a razor edge over this single case.

In other words, would there be rules that could exclude so-called undesirability. And that caused us, in that time, and for quite a time — with respecting this single case — to ponder, what is the more important? The reputation that we shall have? What people shall think? Or is it our charac-ter? And who are we, considering our records? Alcoholism is quite as unlovely; who are we to deny a man his oppor-tunity — any man or woman? And finally the day of reso-lution came and a bunch were sitting in Dr. Bob's living room arguing what to do. Where upon dear, old Bob looked around and blandly said, 'Isn't it time, folks, to ask our-selves, what would the Master do in a situation like this? Would he turn this man away?'

That was the beginning of the AA Tradition 'That any man who has a drinking problem is a member of AA if he says so, not whether we say so.' Now I think that the import of this on the common welfare has already been *stagnate. Because it takes in even more territory than the confines of our fellowship — it takes in the whole world of alcoholics. Their charter to freedom, to join AA is assured. Indeed it was an act in the general welfare."* [3]

In today's world, the term *sex deviate* probably wouldn't be used to identify the man's other addiction, and there are now Twelve Step groups devoted to addressing any number of compulsive behaviors and addictions, including sex addiction. It is to AA's credit that the fellowship has been able to welcome a wide spectrum of people during its many decades of service. Much of this openness stems from the examples of the cofounders, who cast their nets as widely as possible. The main question has always been, "Are you an alcoholic and do you want to stop drinking?"

In that same talk, Barry L. shared another personal experience of when he was answering phones at the AA clubhouse in Manhattan.

7   There came in, sent by a policeman on the corner, a black man. We had, at that time in New York, no black AA members. We had seen a few black people come into the meetings and had tried very hard to befriend them and talk to them, but they left us. They did not stay with us; I think they thought it was too damned white. It wasn't for them.

Well this man said, "The policeman on the corner said maybe you could help me." He was not only black, but he had long blond hair like Veronica Lake. And he was a real artist with makeup; he was beautifully made up. He had strapped to his back his entire worldly belongings, and he said, "I just came out of prison and I am a dope fiend [a phrase then in use], and I am also an alcoholic and I need help desperately."

I was the last person in the world ... [who] knew what to do and I ran around trying to get people to help me, and a great number of them had come to play poker that afternoon. They wouldn't touch this one with a twelve-foot pole, but one marvelous old woman came and sat there for a long time and talked to him. We didn't know where to start — how do you help someone like this who has so many problems? And none of those people could give me the answers.

So I said I'm going to call the person I know who's been sober longest. So I called Bill and said, "Bill, here's the problem." (I got somebody to take the poor guy out and get him a cup of coffee to start with.) And I said, "Here's the problem, this man is here," and I told him exactly what the man looked like, and what the man told us, and I said, "What do we do? He needs all kinds of help."

And Bill was quiet a minute and then he said, "Well now, did you say he is a drunk?"

And I said, "Oh, yes, we can all tell that. Right off the bat we could tell that."

And Bill said, "I think that is the only question we dare ask. It's up to us now to help him." [4]

Unlike Barry L., today's AA members cannot pick up a telephone to call Bill W. for advice. But this is no problem. Well before his death in 1971, Bill prepared a body of writings that are easily accessible to any AA member.

In many of Bill W.'s early recollections of the development of Tradition Three, he made the claim that the foundation office had requested that the groups send in a list of their membership rules. He then said that if all those rules were put into place at once nobody would qualify for membership. Many of the early groups had tremendous fear and anxiety that allowing the wrong person "in" would capsize the ship.

As it turned out, all of those early fears proved to be groundless. Bill noted in *Twelve Steps and Twelve Traditions*, commonly referred to as the Twelve and Twelve:

> *How could we know that thousands of these sometimes frightening people were to make astonishing recoveries and become our greatest workers and intimate friends? Was it credible that A.A. was to have a divorce rate far lower than average? Could we then foresee that troublesome people were to become our principal teachers of patience and tolerance? Could any then imagine a society which would include every conceivable kind of character, and cut across every barrier of race, creed, politics and language with ease?[5]*

At various times, AA groups have reportedly faced the issue of "qualifying" people as alcoholics. One hears curious stories, probably exaggerated, about early AA members who put newcomers through a rigorous interrogation process before accepting them into the group.

But it apparently took considerable experience to arrive at this point. At the First International Convention in Cleveland in 1950, the speaker selected to talk on Tradition Three was Dick S. of Cleveland, Ohio. He and his brother Paul were early Ohio members. Dick shared these thoughts on Tradition Three.

8 Good afternoon folks. Traditions are the result of experience; are the result of habit and precedence. They're historical. . . . My assignment to discuss Step Three recalls some of the earlier days in AA when my friend here established these Traditions which says, "The only requirement for Alcoholics Anonymous membership is the desire to stop drinking.". . . At the outset there was great curiosity as to whether men who had been approached and had decided to come along were eligible for membership. Many cases, committees were formed to look the brother over and see if he qualified; see if he was eligible. After which, he would probably in rare cases, which has been proved, [he] was put on a probationary period for some time. And after he had matriculated, gone through the primary classes, and was able to recite his lessons, he was then given a badge or grip.

Today, and just in passing, sometimes it would be a good idea for some of the elder statesmen to stop and ponder whether they could have passed the test they were imposing on other people. Probably not. Today, the only requirement for membership in AA, which has been established through precedence and historical endeavors, lies wholly and solely within himself and herself. If one wants to join a lodge or a club, they go there with an affirmation to the fact that they want to join. Certainly, who are we to question a man or a woman who comes to us with probably one of the most destructive habits on earth and asks our help by merely signifying that he too wants to go around with us? Thus, I think the Tradition Number Three is not ours to question but to welcome.[6]

Most AA groups today attempt to adhere to Tradition Three by being inclusive of anyone with an alcohol problem wishing to get well. In some regions the groups have mostly "open meetings." These meetings can be attended by anyone, although most group policies request that only AA members share at these meetings. This, however, is a group decision, and the group gets to decide what is best.

In 1951, Bill W. shared this tidbit on the Third Tradition:

> Well you remember the early days [when] we had all those membership rules. Where have they gone now? We're not afraid anymore. We open our arms wide. We say, "We don't care who you are; what your other difficulties are. You just need [to] say, 'I'm an alcoholic, I'm interested' [and] you declare yourself in." Our [early] membership ideas put exactly in reverse.[7]

In 1960, he made the following comments:

Then we have another vital aspect of our charter for liberty that has to do with membership in Alcoholics Anonymous. Few societies or governments there must be, where a person can be a member, a citizen in full standing, the moment he says so. He has to meet conditions. Here there are no conditions. We believe that we should have no first- [and] second-class members. We believe that we should not enforce any obedience, a vast charter of liberty.[8]

Thus, AA experience was already proving that the only sound course for AA was in the simplicity of dropping all rules and regulations, as well as any attempt to "qualify" people as alcoholics. Much of this change for the better can be attributed to Bill's own writings over the years, especially in *Twelve Steps and Twelve Traditions* and *The Language of the Heart*.

A general understanding of alcoholism and Tradition Three will help any open-minded member to understand that to disallow any alcoholic the opportunity for membership into AA, for any reason, could be the equivalent of pronouncing a death sentence. Certainly this is why the founders wanted AA to be all-inclusive and never exclusive.

So the reason AA has Tradition Three is clear: it is a life or death issue. And AA groups do have a spiritual mission to carry the message of recovery to all who suffer from alcoholism.

These important membership issues continue throughout AA today. The fellowship is faced with

growing concerns about alcoholics attending AA meetings and wanting to discuss their "other problems" and
identifying themselves as both an alcoholic and an
addict, for example. Although this may appear to be
related to the Third Tradition, perhaps it will be a more
appropriate topic in the Traditions to follow.

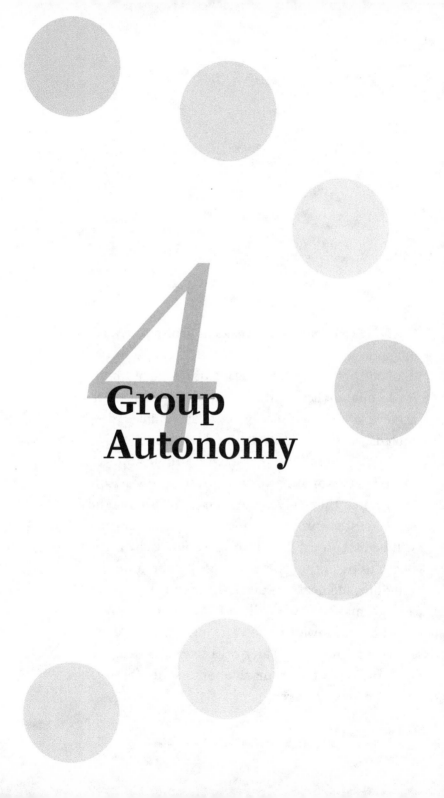

4
Group
Autonomy

The First Tradition speaks of group unity: "Our common welfare should come first; personal recovery depends upon A.A. unity."[1] This principle of humility is essential for self-centered, ego-driven alcoholics to achieve sobriety. The idea of personal humility is deeply rooted in all of AA's Steps and Traditions.

Just as members must give up their ambitious drive for personal power and prestige to stay sober, the groups themselves must also conform to these same spiritual principles and practices or the results will be disastrous. When well-meaning individualists begin to push their personal agenda, be it political, religious, medical, or social, the results will be swift and permanent. As William L. White points out in this book's foreword, the Washingtonians and other many well-meaning early organizations that began with the goal of keeping alcoholics sober fell by the wayside for similar reasons.

Bill W. thought that he might be able to run AA from New York. Considering his business background and legal education, this would seem practical for the cofounder. He had experiences with most of the groups and the group problems. This consideration would seem sensible in most other societies, but as Bill explained in the book *Alcoholics Anonymous Comes of Age*, the groups responded in the following way:

> *"We like what you are doing. Sometimes your suggestions and advice are good. But whether to take you or leave you alone is going to be our decision. Out in the groups, we are going to run our own show. We are not going to have a personal government in New York, or anywhere else. Services, yes. But government, no."*
>
> *Hence, AA's Tradition of group autonomy. It didn't take long to formulate that one. They told us just what they wanted, and that included the right to be wrong.*[2]

Just as the Steps were born out of the experience of the first few members, each Tradition was born out of the experiences of the first few groups. All of the Traditions were originally published in 1946, in what was known as "the long form." The long form of Tradition Four is:

> *With respect to its own affairs, each AA group should be responsible to no other authority than its own conscience. But when its plans concern the welfare of neighboring groups also, those groups ought to be consulted. And no*

group, regional committee, or individual should ever take any action that might greatly affect AA as a whole without conferring with the trustees of the General Service Board. On such issues our common welfare is paramount.[3]

The idea of each group being in charge of, or responsible for, its own affairs and being free to make whatever decisions are seen fit has probably been one of the fellowship's greatest assets over the years. Individual groups tend to work out problems with certain members, such as dealing with those who talk about other problems not related to staying sober, show up intoxicated, or become so disruptive that meetings cannot continue. Of course the Tradition also has a qualification, which simply states "except in matters affecting other groups or AA as a whole."

Since each group has the freedom to conduct itself in whatever manner the collective group conscience decides, AA has no need for a government. The groups are responsible to themselves, and individual sobriety depends upon the common welfare. This Tradition essentially makes it impossible for AA to be or to become a cult.

On several occasions during AA's seventy-six years, the fellowship has received some negative press. It seems that most of these negative reports falsely accuse AA of being a cult. The first negative article appeared in a September 1964 issue of the *Saturday Evening Post*. It was entitled "Alcoholics Can Be Cured—Despite AA" by Dr. Arthur Cain. And printed on the bottom of the front cover was "Down with AA." In the article was the claim "An expert charges that Alcoholics Anonymous has become a dogmatic cult that blocks medical progress and hampers many members' lives."[4]

At the time the author credited AA with 350,000 members and 10,000 chapters (groups). The 2011 estimate is more than 2,000,000 members with 107,976 groups worldwide. Each of these groups is autonomous. There have been groups since AA's earliest days that have displayed behavior and actions that were potentially harmful to other groups and AA as a whole. Unfortunately, when these groups surface they can bring about negative reaction from the community and often some short-lived bad press. Thankfully these groups generally fade away as quickly as they start.

We've all heard the statement "One bad apple spoils the whole barrel." However, with AA, that doesn't seem to fully apply. There are many reasons for this, but mainly it's the result of groups adhering to the Fourth Tradition's principle of group autonomy. As Bill W. stated, this Tradition ensures "each group has the right to be wrong."

The *Washington Post* printed an article in July 2007 entitled "Seeking Recovery, Finding Confusion." The article detailed a group that chose to have a "leader" and disregarded the AA Traditions. In this group there were reports of older men allegedly having sex with teenage girls, young members having to cut ties with families, and assorted other practices supposedly necessary for one to maintain sobriety. The requirements of that group resembled the characteristics of a cult.

From the article:

> Despite a stellar reputation and worldwide brand, it has never been more than a set of bedrock traditions. It has no firm hierarchy, no official regulations, and exercises no oversight of individual groups. Disgruntled former Midtown members discovered this in recent months when they tried to get the central AA office in New York to condemn Midtown's tactics and departures from the traditions, including a highly unusual practice of assigning older men to sponsor young women....
>
> The main office does offer "strong suggestions" for how groups should operate, including how to pair each member with a sponsor who shares confidences and helps the member stay sober. AA recommends that "It's best if a man sponsors a man and a woman sponsors a woman, so that there are not outside distractions," the staffer said.[5]

Since the article appeared in 2007, nothing further can be found regarding this unfortunate situation; it's likely the group disbanded. Alcoholics Anonymous will never completely be free of problems, but a common thread through the fabric of AA is spiritual progress, not perfection. Most group problems are solved within the group, area, or district. In AA's seventy-six years of history as of this writing, there are only a small handful of negative press releases. Considering that there are more than 100,000 groups, that really is a positive testament.

If you think about the fact that these groups are made up of alcoholics in various stages of sobriety, it's even more astonishing.

Implicit in both the Twelve Steps and the Twelve Traditions is the suggestion that each individual member be willing to surrender to something if he or she is to remain sober. The paradox is that this is how the members achieve sobriety. Each member is unique with a variety of experiences, and each group is unique in providing different opportunities to sacrifice, to give back. At the group level, one person might have to sacrifice his or her need to control a situation or manage people, while another person might have to sacrifice personal comfort by extending a helping hand to a new member. One group might provide this opportunity by holding meetings in jails or prisons, while another puts a greater emphasis on assigning members to help newcomers feel welcomed. This responsibility falls under the heading of service.

Both of AA's cofounders understood the necessity and the benefits of service. Bill W., when speaking about the very early days, quoted Dr. Bob as saying, "Don't you think it's time we find another alcoholic to work on?" This simple statement of service has grown throughout the AA community to the point that today, when a new member comes to a meeting, it is suggested that he or she join a home group, get a sponsor, and find a service commitment.

Each group has various service positions available for members. Most groups set these services up on a rotating basis; therefore one person doesn't undertake all of the responsibility. The groups' structures resemble one another; however, the Fourth Tradition gives the group freedom to conduct its business in accordance with the conscience of that group. For example, there are many different types of AA meetings: open, closed, speaker, discussion, beginner, workshop, Step study, Big Book focus, and so on. This is a decision made by the group.

As we discussed in the previous chapter on Tradition Three, the idea of having AA meetings specific to a particular group of members has been somewhat controversial since these groups first began springing up in 1941. The argument stems from the idea that these special groups are being exclusive, rather than inclusive, that they do not adhere to the Third Tradition, "The only requirement for A.A. membership is a desire to stop drinking."[6] At first glance, this argument seems to have some merit, and these groups do appear to be in conflict with the Third Tradition. However the Fourth Tradition clearly provides each group with the privilege of making these decisions.

Barry L., quoted in the previous chapter in a talk from 1985, spoke of a heated debate that had taken place at the conference regarding the inclusion of gay and lesbian groups in the AA directory. The conference approved the inclusion, and afterward somebody spoke up and said, "I want to propose a resolution that it is the sense of the conference that no AA group anywhere, of any kind, should ever turn away a newcomer from his or her first meeting."[7] It passed unanimously. This resolution, supporting the Third Tradition, calms the fears held by some that new members reaching out for help might be turned away because they don't "fit" with that particular group.

The autonomy guaranteed by the Fourth Tradition is also bolstered by the Second Tradition. Many AA groups, in addition to having a regularly scheduled business meeting, conduct a "group inventory." This practice allows group members the opportunity to examine the policies and procedures of their group. This is how many groups allow for the ultimate authority, a loving God, to express Himself in the group conscience. This also gives the group the freedom to be truly autonomous, and for the conduct of each group to be in accordance with the Second Tradition.

Historically speaking, there seem to be few issues that are new. Most of the concerns that members have can be resolved, in time, through the group conscience and respecting group autonomy. One of the concerns is that the number of atheist/agnostic groups is increasing, and will somehow affect the common welfare of AA. When Bill W. wrote the book *Alcoholics Anonymous,* he addressed concerns facing atheists and agnostics in the chapter "We Agnostics." He wrote the following.

> *To one who feels he is an atheist or agnostic such an experience seems impossible, but to continue as he is means disaster, especially if he is an alcoholic of the hopeless*

variety. To be doomed to an alcoholic death or to live on a spiritual basis are not always easy alternatives to face.

But it isn't so difficult. About half our original fellowship were exactly that type.[8]

The implication here is that half of the original members were atheist/agnostic, and this didn't seem to create any concerning issue. If anything, Bill W. wanted that door to be left wide open. When the Fourth Tradition was written, the pioneering members were very much aware of the potential problems that could arise in the fellowship when each group was given the authority to be a separate and complete entity of its own. When this Fourth Tradition was presented at the First International Conference, Dick S. shared the following.

[9] Number four says, "Each group should be autonomous except in matters affecting other groups or AA as a whole." Brother, in Cleveland we've had autonomy. Some years ago, some efforts were made there to propose the opening of a downtown central office, which meant bringing that idea before the entire membership for approval and, incidentally, a little money.

And the gentleman who was trying his best to spread the cause was denied the privilege of talking to his fellow members in several of the Cleveland groups. Now there is autonomy. Printed material was prepared. Some of the groups would not allow it displayed or to be given to their followers. There's autonomy. Nevertheless, again, a small measure of history was being born, but because [of the]

various [groups'] autonomy, the groups could not prevent their members from interchanging. But the word
got around anyhow. The office was opened, and it served
seven successful years. It performed a tremendous, but
vital service in Cleveland.

You see that this activity was for all of Cleveland, but
a few members decided it shouldn't be. But the will of the
entire membership was finally heard, and resulted in this
successful endeavor. Now everything that has gone before
has created everything we do. This meeting and every
other meeting, everything we do is based on some prec-
edent; by now, fifteen years' worth. And perhaps we are
ready to recognize that Traditions have become habit.[9]

Today, most large metropolitan areas have hundreds of AA groups, with some areas having thousands
of meetings weekly. It is doubtful that each group would
consult with the other groups in their decision making
about meeting times, changes in format, workshops,
group picnics, and other various functions, even when
these things could possibly affect a neighboring group.
Most large cities have an intergroup or central office
that handles this type of communication for the groups.
These central offices help the groups by assisting in
coordinating activities within their particular service
area. These support services help the AA groups to be
autonomous without negatively affecting other groups,
or AA as a whole.

The central offices are not a part of AA's general
service structure. They provide needed services to

the groups they serve. These offices are supported by donations from the groups in their area. Many of them also sell AA books and literature.

While every AA group has the right to conduct itself as it is guided through the group conscience, it is suggested that when a group is making a decision that will concern the general welfare of AA or other groups it should first consult those groups that might be affected. If the action will affect AA as a whole, the trustees of the General Service Board should be consulted.

According to an editorial in the March 1948 *A.A. Grapevine:*

> *This Tradition, Number 4, is a specific application of general principles already outlined in Traditions 1 and 2. Tradition 1 states,* "Each member of Alcoholics Anonymous is but a small part of a great whole. A.A. must continue to live or most of us will surely die. Hence our common welfare comes first. But individual welfare follows close afterward." *Tradition 2 states,* "For our group purpose there is but one ultimate authority — a loving God as He may express Himself in our group conscience."
>
> *With these concepts in mind, let us look more closely at Tradition 4. The first sentence of Tradition 4 guarantees each A.A. group local autonomy. With respect to its own affairs, the group may make any decisions, adopt any attitudes that it likes. No over-all or intergroup authority should challenge this primary privilege. We feel this ought to be so, even though the group might sometimes act with complete indifference, to our*

tradition. For example, an A.A. *group could, if it wished, hire a paid preacher and support him out of the proceeds of a group night club. Though such an absurd procedure would be miles outside our tradition, the group's "right to be wrong" would be held inviolate. We are sure that each group can be granted, and safely granted, these most extreme privileges. We know that our familiar process of trial and error would summarily eliminate both the preacher and the night club. Those severe growing pains which invariably follow any radical departure from* A.A. *tradition can be absolutely relied upon to bring an erring group back into line. An* A.A. *group need not be coerced by any human government over and above its own members. Their own experience, plus* A.A. *opinion in surrounding groups, plus God's prompting in their group conscience would be sufficient. Much travail has already taught us this. Hence we may confidently say to each group, "You should be responsible to no other authority than your own conscience."*

Yet please note one important qualification. It will be seen that such extreme liberty of thought and action applies only to the group's own affairs. Rightly enough, this Tradition goes on to say, "But when its plans concern the welfare of neighboring groups also, those groups ought to be consulted." *Obviously, if any individual, group or regional committee could take an action which might seriously affect the welfare of Alcoholics Anonymous as a whole, or seriously disturb surrounding groups, that would not be liberty at all. It would be sheer license; it would be anarchy, not democracy.*

Group Autonomy

Therefore, we A.A.s have universally adopted the principle of consultation. This means that if a single A.A. group wishes to take any action which might affect surrounding groups, it consults them. Or, if there be one, it confers with the intergroup committee for the area. Likewise, if a group or regional committee wishes to take any action that might affect A.A. as a whole, it consults the trustees of The Alcoholic Foundation, who are, in effect, our overall General Service Committee. For instance, no group or intergroup could feel free to initiate, without consultation, any publicity that might affect A.A. as a whole. Nor could it assume to represent the whole of Alcoholics Anonymous by printing and distributing anything purporting to be A.A. standard literature. This same principle would naturally apply to all similar situations. Though there is no formal compulsion to do so, all undertakings of this general character are customarily checked with our A.A. General Headquarters.

This idea is clearly summarized in the last sentence of Tradition Four, which observes, "On such issues our common welfare is paramount."[10]

We've already alluded to the fact that today — as more people are celebrating their cultural, sexual, and racial identities — thousands of AA groups have formed to reflect people's desire to be with others who share their unique life experiences. Especially in larger cities, you'll find groups made up of mostly gays, lesbians, men, women, Native Americans, Latinos, and even groups of people from the same profession — for example flight attendants, doctors, or lawyers. And if you go to a different meeting every night, you're likely to find one group reading the Big Book, another going through the Steps, and yet another allowing the rotating group leader to pick the topic for discussion. But in the end, all of these groups share a single purpose, and that is to help any alcoholic who still suffers — which takes us to the Fifth Tradition.

5

Why the Shoemaker Should Stick to His Last

From its early beginnings, AA's Twelve Step program was recognized as a possible solution for many human problems other than alcoholism. Since AA groups were so effective in dealing with the centuries-old malady of alcoholism, why couldn't the fellowship open its doors to sufferers of all kinds? Why couldn't all victims of compulsive illnesses meet in one place to handle many problems at one time?

According to Bill W., this was a bad idea, and the Fifth Tradition discourages putting it into practice: "Each group has but one primary purpose—to carry its message to the alcoholic who still suffers."[1] Bill was so firm in this belief that he used an old axiom to explain it: "Shoemaker, stick to thy last."[2] He would say that it's better to do one thing supremely well than to do many things badly.[3] This also simplified what should qualify a person to be an AA member. One needs only ask if the person is an alcoholic and has a desire to quit drinking.

Yet, in observing AA in action, some feel the groups can take on other responsibilities. In one midwestern city for example, a local citizen became concerned that ex-convicts often had no safe place to hang out in their spare time. Though he was not an AA member, he was certain that the ideal place would be the building that the local AA group leased on a full-time basis. As he saw it, the warmth and friendship shown by AA members in their meetings would aid the ex-convicts in adjusting to life outside prison.

Although a few of the local members had served time in prison, there was simply no support for this proposal. While meetings were open to ex-convicts who belonged to AA, the group would have diluted its efforts by accepting a second purpose of providing a haven for individuals who were not in the fellowship. Whatever the merits of such a proposal, it was clearly outside AA's mission of helping alcoholics.

AA groups dealt with other proposals that went above and beyond the primary purpose of helping alcoholics. The late Nell Wing, who was Bill W.'s secretary for many years and later became AA's archivist, noted in her biography that

> *Bill, like the earlier members, did not approve of multipurpose groups or of drug addicts without alcoholic problems participating as members in AA closed meetings.*[4]

Fortunately, AA has made it possible for other fellowships to use the Twelve Steps in working with problems other than alcohol. In fact, Nell believed that

Bill's openness to sharing AA principles, AA's Twelve Steps, and AA's experience with other Twelve Step Fellowships must be regarded as one of his most far-reaching contributions.[5]

It likely started with his recognition of the need for groups focusing on family to have their own separate fellowship. He encouraged Lois to organize this fellowship, which became the Al-Anon Family Groups.

As with all of AA's Traditions, Bill not only used the experiences of the original groups, but he also leaned upon the experiences of other societies. He used many examples of the Washingtonian Society when he discussed various Traditions. Bill recognized that the downfall of the Washingtonians could be directly linked to their lack of focus on a primary purpose. He knew that this society had once held fast to its original purpose of helping the drunkard to recover and had done so quite successfully. Eventually, however, the group's members found themselves mired in a variety of outside issues, which eventually led to the group's demise.

Maybe it was wisdom or perhaps fear that caused Bill and the other pioneers to safeguard AA's future when they decided that AA could have but one primary purpose. Of course, in the very early days when the unnamed society began showing results with alcoholics, there were thoughts that these principles could be used to save the world from all of its ills.

At the Texas State Convention in June 1954, Bill shared some ideas that were discussed:

So, on this late fall afternoon in 1937, Smithy and I were
10 talking together in his living room; Anne sitting there by
the gas logs. And we began to count noses. How many
people had stayed dry: in Akron, in New York, and maybe
a few in Cleveland? How many had stayed dry and for
how long? And when we added up that score, sure it was
a handful—I don't know, thirty-five [to] forty maybe. But
enough time had elapsed on enough really fatal cases of
alcoholism, so that when we grasped the import of these
small statistics, Bob and I saw for the first time that this
thing was going to succeed. That God in his providence
and mercy had thrown a new light into the dark caves
where we and our kind had been, and were still by the
millions dwelling.

I never can forget the elation and ecstasy that seized
us both. And then we fell happily talking and reflecting;
we reflected that, well, a couple of score of them were
sober, but this had taken three long years. There had been
an immense amount of failure, but a long time had been
taken just to sober up the handful. How could this handful carry its message to all those who still didn't know?
Not all the drunks in the world could come to Akron or to
New York.

How could we transmit our message to them; by
what means? Maybe, we thought, we should go to the
old-timers in each group, but that meant nearly everybody, to find the sum of money—somebody else's money,
of course—and say to them, "Well now, take a sabbati-
cal year off your job if you have any, and go to Kentucky,
Omaha, Chicago, San Francisco, and Los Angeles and

wherever it may be and you give this thing a year and get a group started."

It had already gotten evident by then that we were just about to be moved out of the City Hospital in Akron to make room for people with broken legs and ailing livers, that the hospitals were not too happy with us. We tried to run their business perhaps too much, and besides, drunks were apt to be noisy in the night and there were other inconveniences, which were all tremendous. So, it was obvious that, drunks being such unlovely creatures, we would have to have a great chain of hospitals. And as that dream burst upon me, it sounded good, because you see, I'd been down in Wall Street in the promotion business and I remember the great sums of money that were made as soon as people got this chain idea. You know, the chain drug store, the chain grocery store, or the chain dry goods store. Why not chain drunk tanks, and let us make the dollar? So we needed some missionaries, subsidized. We needed a chain of drunk tanks; that got very clear, awful clear to me. Bob was a conservative type of Yankee; I don't think he was quite so fast for those items. But I was very interested. It would take a pile of dough to finance all this, but after all, with this brand-new light shining in our dark world, we'd just squirt it in the eye of the rich guys and they'd up with the dough. Besides, we reflected, we'd have to get some kind of literature.[6]

He went on to say that even then he and Bob had realized that they couldn't be the government of Alcoholics Anonymous.

He, I guess more than I, already realized that the conscience of the group — the opinion of the group — when it
was an informed opinion and in the group's interests, could
be better than our own.[7]

That very evening they got the Akron Group
together at the home of a nonalcoholic couple there in
Akron. Bill said there were eighteen in attendance and
the group listened to his pitch for missionaries, drunk
tanks, and a book. After some debate about involving
money in the deal and possibly making it too professional, the group voted to have Bill go back to New York
and raise the money for the book. In another talk, Bill
said that he was to write the book and raise the money,
while Dr. Bob was investigating the possibility of the
drunk tanks.

The AA Traditions were not yet written, but some of
the ideas were brought to light that evening in Akron.
The group understood that if they had no literature, their
ability to carry the message would be greatly hampered.

The decision made in Akron that October evening
in 1937 led Bill directly to John D. Rockefeller Jr., where
he had hoped the money issue would be solved forever.
Mr. Rockefeller was intrigued by Bill and the other New
York members. He asked Frank Amos, who was associated with a group of advisers for Mr. Rockefeller on his
charitable decisions, to look into this matter further. Mr.
Amos traveled to Akron in 1938 and met with the group
members there. He also investigated Dr. Bob — AA at
this time was still a nameless society. Upon returning to

New York, Mr. Amos presented his favorable findings to Rockefeller. After personally reviewing how AA worked, Mr. Rockefeller came to the conclusion that too much money might spoil this thing. He made a relatively small donation and began sponsoring annual dinners on AA's behalf. (Later on, when AA became more fully self-supporting, the society sent Rockefeller a letter thanking him for his help and assuring him that AA could now meet its own financial obligations.)

As groups began spreading across the country, there were ideas for AA hospitals, health farms, clubhouses, and so on. The founders suggested and insisted that although many of these services are good and helpful to suffering alcoholics, they could not use the AA name. Cooperation without affiliation is the guiding principle. Because of these suggested policies, AA was then, and still is, able today to focus the attention of the group on one purpose and one purpose only—helping the alcoholic to find and maintain sobriety.

In the transcription from the Cleveland International Convention, Gene from Toledo opted to discuss Traditions Five and Six. When discussing Tradition Six, he told a story about an opportunity for the AA center in his community to operate a hospital for local alcoholics, which is shared in the following chapter. Here are his thoughts on Tradition Five:

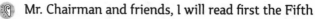 Mr. Chairman and friends, I will read first the Fifth
11 Tradition: "Each group has but one primary purpose—to carry its message to the alcoholic who still suffers." Well,

of course the message referred to here, as you know, is the messy job; our program of recovery, the Twelve Steps of AA. The Twelve Steps contain the substance of Alcoholics Anonymous; the spirit of Alcoholics Anonymous. Perhaps what we are discussing this afternoon has more to do with the form than the substance. But as you know in all human endeavors, it is necessary to have a vehicle, an instrumentality, an organism of some sort through which an activity, particular one of the spiritual nature, may be conveyed.

You know, they played a trick on me this afternoon and told me that I was restricted to five minutes; I'd say that's a hell of a trick to play on a lawyer. Especially when we're all talking even after fifteen years about a subject on which none of us profess to be authorities. I'm reminded a little of the story I heard the other day of the weekly meeting of the Boy Scout troop, in which the boys were to report on their good deeds for the week. And one of them got up before the Scout Master and said, "Johnny and Phil and Teri and I helped an old lady across the street." The scout master said, "Well, how come it took three of you?" Johnny said, "The old lady didn't want to go."

And perhaps that is quite apropos of what we're discussing here. I remember in my early reading of the Big Book, something stood out in Bill's story about the destruction of self-centeredness, the abnegation of self, which he found necessary in order to recover from alcoholism, and which the good Dr. Silkworth said he tried to bring about. The change he tried to bring about in those that came to him.

And so I'm suggesting this afternoon in my view of the subject of the Traditions and particularly this one, that each of us individually and each of us in our groups must stand ready to renounce self; to be willing to abandon that which seems to be fallacious, and which might be detrimental to the greater good of all. Each group has but one primary purpose — to carry its message to the alcoholic who still suffers. "Well," you ask me, "What other purpose could there be?"

We all know very well the deductive detours that may be offered to any AA group. There are many ramifications of AA, many of which have merit. For instance, the cultivation of social life and activity in itself is a laudable thing. We have long since had our customs, you might say, of anniversaries, perhaps group anniversaries, summer picnics. And in our own community, we have AA frolic and fun of all decent kinds. But I think we can recognize that that phase of our activity might be overemphasized.

A particular group might very well gain a reputation as a bunch of good fellows who throw good parties. But wouldn't it be a better test of the success of that group to measure ... [its] growth in alcoholic souls that are helped toward recovery through the activity of that group? Sometimes I think the word *spiritual* is misleading to some of us in AA. We treat it as synonymous with the word *religious,* and I don't believe it is. I'm merely suggesting it's my opinion that we would have a better understanding of the word *spiritual* if we would apply it to everyday life. There are positive, good, spiritual characteristics and there are negative ones. In our own circles, we'll speak of someone as being; there's a fellow who's loyal, there's a fellow who's devoted, there's a man who is energetic. Of a soldier, he's a brave man. Of a worker, he's industrious, he's on the job, he's capable. And all of those adjectives that I have used denote and connote spiritual qualities. The opposite of those things we all know.

They may be vices; they may be even some of the deadly sins. So I think when we speak of our groups as being spiritual entities, we can understand them better in that light when we say that the only excuse the group has for its existence, for its continued operation, and the only measure of its effectiveness is carrying the message, and the message is the content and the understanding of the Twelve Steps of recovery.[8]

Beginners in AA learn very quickly that once they get sober they must "Give it away to keep it." This is one of the guiding principles in AA. Bill W., when recalling his personal story of his last visit to Towns Hospital, mentions that his visitor (Ebby) suggested that he should practice these newly acquired principles in all of his affairs and be willing to pass them on to the next man. These ideas came directly from the Oxford Group Ebby had been attending and through which he had found his sobriety. These principles were to become the Twelfth Step in the AA program, to "carry this message to [other] alcoholics."

Many sober alcoholics say that when they were presented with the facts about the hopelessness of their situation by someone who really knew, another alcoholic who could identify with their situation, they found hope and were easily convinced that they too could get well. One anonymous AA member shares this story about his early days in sobriety:

> I was living with my sponsor because I had nowhere else to go. On this particular evening I had remembered that I should be honest, so I said to my sponsor, "I'm not going to the meeting tonight!" The sponsor replied, "Oh, why not?" Being honest, I said, "Well it's the same bunch of guys saying the same thing, and I want to take the night off and watch a ballgame." The sponsor looked up and said, "You don't go to AA to get, you go to AA to give!" He went on and explained to the new man that there may be a brand new person at the meeting tonight and when the new person sees him as an example of AA (sober), for just that limited period of time, he might find hope and comfort enough to stay sober for the day and to come back the next.[9]

It is this kind of unselfish giving that brings about a psychic change that is mentioned in the Big Book. If the AA group or member had to have some other qualifications to carry the message, or if AA had any other purpose, the effectiveness of the message would be diminished, and the sick man or woman would likely die. Bill talked about this in the Twelve and Twelve.

The unique ability of each A.A. to identify himself with, and bring recovery to, the newcomer in no way depends upon his learning, eloquence, or on any special individual skills. The only thing that matters is that he is an alcoholic who has found a key to sobriety.[10]

The Fifth Tradition is to the group what the Twelfth Step is to the individual. Many stories have been handed down through the years, and certainly there are different variations of the same story. A longtime member shared this story:

> We always went in twos when making a Twelve Step call. This particular day nobody was available to go except a new guy with only five days of sobriety. When we entered the drunk's home, I said, "I'll do the talking." And talk I did, for at least an hour. Finally the drunk interrupted me and looked at the new man saying, "How long have you been sober?" The kid responded with, "Only five days." The drunk looked back at him and said, "Please tell me — how'd you do it?" [11]

6

Stability through Sacrifice

Historically speaking, the Sixth Tradition has probably been tested more than any other Tradition. Even today, AA is faced with potential problems from well-meaning members wanting to tie the AA name to some outside enterprise.

The early days were filled with everything, from AA club houses to "drying out farms." Advertising and promotion companies wanted to capitalize on AA's good name by recruiting sober members as their spokespersons. When the Sixth Tradition first appeared in the long form, it read as follows:

Problems of money, property, and authority may easily divert us from our primary spiritual aim. We think, therefore, that any considerable property of genuine use to A.A. should be separately incorporated and managed, thus dividing the material from the spiritual. An A.A. group, as such, should never go into business. Secondary aids to

A.A., such as clubs or hospitals which require much property or administration, ought to be incorporated and so set apart that, if necessary, they can be freely discarded by the groups. Hence such facilities ought not to use the A.A. name. Their management should be the sole responsibility of those people who financially support them. For clubs, A.A. managers are usually preferred. But hospitals, as well as other places of recuperation, ought to be well outside A.A.— and medically supervised. While an A.A. group may cooperate with anyone, such cooperation ought never go so far as affiliation or endorsement, actual or implied. An A.A. group can bind itself to no one.[1]

In 1950, this Tradition was presented to the fellowship in its current form — known today as the short form. It had only the slightest modifications, which eliminated some verbiage. The principles contained in the Tradition were still there, perhaps even more clearly than originally presented. The Tradition now simply reads:

An AA group ought never endorse, finance, or lend the AA name to any related facility or outside enterprise, lest problems of money, property, and prestige divert us from our primary purpose.[2]

In the previous chapter we discussed in detail the primary purpose of the group. When examining the Traditions, it is easy to conclude that Bill could have combined several of them and reduced the number from twelve to as few as six or seven. Bill seemed to favor the idea of using the number *twelve* when stressing important issues or presenting certain concepts to the fellowship. He first used this with the Twelve Steps, then of course with the Twelve Traditions, and in 1962 with the Twelve Concepts.

AA faced some early challenges when Marty M., one of the first women in AA, formed the National Council on Alcoholism and Drug Dependency. (It was then called the National Council for Education on Alcoholism, NCEA.) Marty prepared, signed, and sent out a solicitation letter that stated that AA would benefit from any contributions received. This put Bill in the spotlight, according to Nell Wing, because Marty was a personal friend and he strongly believed in what she was trying to accomplish. He had loyally and publicly endorsed her efforts, Nell wrote, as well as her anonymity break. Both Bill's and Dr. Bob's names appeared on the NCEA letterhead! There was also a pamphlet printed that listed both of them on the NCEA advisory board. An uproar from the AA membership followed. Bill and Dr. Bob realized that they had made a mistake and had their names withdrawn from the letterhead.[3] Marty also cooperated in making sure that there was no affiliation between AA and the NCEA.

Bill cautioned AA enthusiasts about linking the AA name to anything other than straight AA service. He recognized that many AA members who were also great promoters in the business world would see the benefit of tying the AA name to their cause or occupation. Throughout his life, he discouraged members from any activities that would link AA to outside enterprises, regardless of how good some of these opportunities appeared to be.

Certainly he knew that many of these services and the AA members associated with them were doing great work. But experience and wisdom dictated that the policy must be no endorsement in name or financial association with any related or unrelated outside enterprise.

At the 1960 AA International Convention, Bill went into more detail on this subject:

> We were talking about the relation with outside agencies in the field of alcohol.... We can learn a lot from [clergymen]...about the soul and its ailments. We can learn a lot from the psychiatrists and psychologists about the ailments of the emotions. Then there come the ailments of the body, which accompany [alcoholism]...Now, how are we going to be related to all of these people who, under the hope that we have given them, are laboring each in their several ways to mitigate this dire illness upon which we have made only the merest strides? Shall we be loud in condemnations of the medical profession when some new drug comes out that gives us the heebie-jeebies? We ain't mad at the distillers, we don't drink their wares, we don't have to take the pills even though they're good for other people, do we? So why slug new attempts to mitigate the body ills of people? Let us be wide open, let's be friendly. Let us take a firm stance when we know what we're talking about and let us be filled with eager and hopeful

expectancy otherwise. I think we can do that; there isn't any danger; friendliness is not very expensive. Then this illness of the emotions; . . . in our board of trustees, sits a psychiatrist who has held up the hands of this movement from its beginning, when it was costly and took great courage, great understanding, and great humility to do so. He got me to read a paper before the New York State Medical Association, before the American Psychiatrist Association.

I'll never forget that great annual meeting in Montreal. Maybe nine out of ten of the people in that room who heard my curbstone opinions as a stockbroker about alcoholism, and I added with trimmings that great illumination with the roman candles and things. I don't believe nine out of ten took the slightest stock in what I was saying, this was so far from where they are. Their conditioning in mind had been so different, but they did one thing that we often fail to do: they tried hard to see what was there. And they had seen recoveries and they asked themselves what this meant and they accorded me something that we too often do not accord to them. They accorded to this society respect, an effort to understand. And even though they differed with us as to what happens, they knew that plenty was going on that was good and that we could often do what they couldn't do. And in their humility, and we prayed about our own, they said, "Yes, publish this talk in our magazine; take it out of there as a pamphlet, and show it worldwide to psychiatrists everywhere." This was one of the most moving examples of humility, in a corridor where humility can come hard, that I have ever seen.

I once did some pieces called "Let's be Friendly with our Friends." I guess most people agreed that this was a good idea, but some people said we have certain friends that "I'll be goddamned that I want to be friendly with." But, why not? Now, okay, we've got another classy thing. We've got some state efforts around, rehabilitation things. We got some private efforts; some of them are good, some of them are fairly good, some of them lousy, just like AA groups are. As a society, we are a decade older than they are. They are in the trial-and-error process, and we attack these people when they use the AA name, when I think we should really educate them.

We should educate the public, that AA can't offer its endorsements, only its friendliness and cooperation where this is mutually possible. There isn't any point in attacking people who pretty generally are dedicated. Sure, in these agencies there are folks with an eye to the main chance but have we no members in Alcoholics Anonymous who are not having an eye on the main chance?

There was a time that we could have been fearful, that these enterprises would be tempted to use our name for purposes of raising money; for purposes of getting publicity; and for the purposes of bringing matrimony between us for education, research, and rehabilitation. There was a genuine cause, let us not say for fear, but for concern and apprehension. In those days we were pretty small, but today, the Tradition of Alcoholics Anonymous is a thing of far greater power than any law. We know that its protection is something that we need. And these people are learning about [it], learning to respect it, and the public is learning about it and learning to respect it. And those, who in carelessness, eagerness, willfulness, try to make a public use of it, well they are finding that it is unprofitable.

We don't have to get sore or fear these people. We just say this is the part of a growing-up process, and you must remember that these agencies are approached and will be approached in increasing numbers by alcoholics who are afraid of coming in here for fear they're "God bitten" or something. Therefore, our friendliness with those agencies, tempered only by our insistence that they don't use the AA name in public to further their interests, ought to be very freely and warmly given. They are channels of communication to these uncounted millions that we haven't even got to and can be increasingly so.

No matter how much politics or money is wasted, or how many swell jobs, or how many vested interests are established, all of this is the history and grief of the evolution of something. Let us look at this with calmness and equanimity. Surely our strength among ourselves is so great that no one or any number of these agencies could possibly be the tail that wags the AA dog. Isn't that so?[4]

Bill's wisdom and understanding of how important AA's cooperation was with various organizations and agencies would have its long-term benefits. One result of this attitude can be seen today in meetings throughout the United States, with the relationship between the courts and AA. Another is with relationships between treatment facilities and AA.

A great number of AA members have been directed to AA through courts and treatment centers. AA welcomes these members, provided that the individual meets AA's standards for membership as stated in Tradition Three. Of course, this is often a sensitive and sometimes controversial issue, because it's difficult to measure whether the individual has a desire to stop drinking, or is only attending the meetings because he or she is court ordered.

Each AA group can deal with these issues as its members see fit. Many groups read a statement at the beginning of each meeting explaining the procedures, so all new members and visitors have an understanding of what is expected. Some groups ask all in attendance to identify themselves as "alcoholic" before the meeting begins. If the meeting is "closed" and there are nonalcoholics present, they are asked to leave and are invited to attend an "open" meeting. Many larger cities have a variety of meeting types, which include both open and closed meetings.

The main idea, as it relates to this particular Tradition, is that the groups avoid developing a relationship that creates an endorsement or affiliation with an outside enterprise. One example would be if the AA group meets in the basement of a particular church. The group would pay rent for the room and should be treated as a tenant. Because AA has no affiliation with the church, it should not be listed as a service provided by the church. This requires that the AA group cooperate with and educate the "landlord" (oftentimes a church secretary) about the AA Tradition of no endorsement. Some churches and newspapers list the AA meeting times and location; this is fine in the spirit of cooperation as long as they don't list it as, for example, "Catholic Church AA Meeting."

AA groups often carry our message into institutions, which include hospitals, jails, and treatment centers. These are services provided by the AA groups. More often these services fall under the AA service structure. In most service areas, a "coordinator" is elected to the service position and accepts volunteers to participate in these special services.

All of these service activities help both AA members and groups to carry their message to those alcoholics who need and want sobriety. The Traditions allow for these relationships, provided that there is no affiliation. AA's Traditions suggest cooperation with these outside agencies.

In a recent interview, a longtime member, Tom I., who has dedicated much of his sober life in AA to working inside prisons, told me the following stories as a commentary on the Sixth Tradition.

> While all of the Traditions over the years have come to have more and more meaning for me, that's certainly true of Six. When I first started looking at that Tradition and appreciate the value of the Traditions, that one was illusive because it sounded like it was dealing at corporate level. It was like it was going to regard the purchasing of buildings, and it certainly includes that, but that is not the

heart of it to me. And as I got to really looking at that and understanding it, from my perspective what I saw was its extremely valuable personal principle. Not everybody has seen or had the experience of seeing what it's like to be owned by what you own. So it's true of money, property, prestige, or anything that starts to own me; mentally, physically, spiritually is an enemy. When I look at the Sixth Tradition, what I'm looking at is a very strong reminder that I don't need to be owned by stuff. And I don't have to have stuff.

I can give a couple of examples, maybe two or three that I'd rather talk about; experiences, examples, then philosophy, and all that kind of stuff. I was down in Texas a little while back, as I seem to be a lot. This took place out in the woods, where I saw there was a guy. I couldn't tell it was a guy, but also sitting there was a beautiful Jaguar, just an absolutely beautiful machine.

When I began looking it over, I realized he had a vanity plate on the front that said, "Step Nine." I was intrigued by that. So I tracked down the cowboy and asked him if that was his car. He proudly said, "Yeah, yeah that's mine, it's a really great car." I said, "I bet it is. Tell me about that vanity plate that you have on the front of it." He replied, "Oh I'm glad you noticed, that is just expressing my appreciation for what's been given to me, and that Jag is among those things. It really represents what the amends process is about because that's really making amends to me." I said, "Well, that's an interesting concept, but I'm afraid that for me it has little to do with Step Nine when I'm looking at what I have."

My purpose in making amends is to straighten out my relationship with the world around me. So I said, "For me, you may call it whatever you want to, but I see it as just sort of an expression of the fact that you've got some bucks. You know that you can afford to buy a car and that's nothing to do with amends that I can see." It was one thing, that Jag had become so dominant in his thinking that he related it to the amends process. An amends is anything but amending to myself. It deals with the Sixth Tradition because it's about allowing money, property, and prestige to become my god. They become where my heart is — in those things. And it can just absolutely do a lot of damage.

There are two other examples that really say it to me. There was a man I didn't know, I met him at a conference some time ago. He asked if I would come speak at his anniversary [meeting] in [a] nearby state. [I] said, "Well sure, I'll be glad to if it's sometime that I can, just let me know when." He called me up several months later and said, "Okay, I'm ready." I said, "Okay, what for?"

He said, "To have you down here." I replied, "Well, when is that?" He followed up by saying, "It's my anniversary and you'll recall that you told me you would speak at my anniversary." And I said, "When?" He told me, and my response was "I'm sorry buddy, but I can't do that." "But you told me you would," he replied, and I said, "I didn't give you my calendar for a year; I told you I would if I could. The fact is I have another commitment." I had already planned to go to my son's pinewood derby race — where a kid is supposed to build a little wooden car and have racing competitions. I told him if he made it to the state finals, I would make it my business to be there with him. And sure enough, he did. He made it to the state finals. And that was my commitment.

So the guy called me and I told him I couldn't do it. He was so adamant that I had to come, and that everything was laid out; that they had killed the calf, and all sorts of stuff. He said that I just had to come. I said, "I'm sorry but I just simply can't." His response was, "Let me see what I can do." He called me back a couple hours later. I told him that it was a daytime commitment I had. He said, "Can you be at the Southern Pines Airport by 6:30?" I said, "Yeah I can make that, it won't be a problem. Why?" He said, "Just be there and we'll take it from there."

So I went back home and drove over to the airport. This was before 9/11. There was not even security present. So everybody knew each other at the airport; they were opening doors. You'd have thought the president was coming. They said, "Come on through, go right on out on the runway."

I wondered, "What on earth is going on?" So I stepped outside. Sitting there was a running helicopter. I said, "Oh my God, this is unreal." It was as if they were carrying an atomic bomb: "Get on board," they demanded. So I got on, and the thing bounced all the way to South Carolina. That was the roughest ride I had ever experienced in my life.

When I finally arrived and went straight from the airport to the podium to speak, I was still vibrating from the helicopter ride and I rattled onto the podium. Eventually I got settled down, and got it done. The next day I went back to the airport, got on the beloved helicopter; we went a short distance and all at once he slam-dunked it. I said, "Why in the devil did you slam-dunk the...[helicopter]?" He said, "I didn't, we crashed." Basically, it sort of let itself down. But we slam-dunked that thing down, scrambled around, and found another helicopter to use.

You can tell from this story, I was dealing with a high roller who had access to this kind of stuff. Finally I got back on another plane to Southern Pines. When I got off, he handed me an envelope. "What is that?" I asked.

"Just a thank you card from the group," he said. "Okay, fine," I replied, and I stuck it in my pocket. When I got home, I pulled out the envelope and inside was a stack of money. I was hot; I gave him time to get back to South Carolina, and then called him.

"What's the deal with the money you had stuck in the envelope you gave me?" He replied, "Yeah, we wanted to reimburse you and cover all of your troubles." I said, "Let me tell you something, Jack (Jack wasn't his name), this is Alcoholics Anonymous and we don't do that type of junk here. I'm not for sale. I don't care what the price is. Don't you ever do this to anybody else." Well, that guy never had another anniversary; you can well imagine there is no short way through the Traditions for me. You can see what money did to this guy. All of his money and affluence had brought him nothing but disaster. It had taken him away from any spiritual core and life. It just ended up so tragically. Then I had another experience right here in my area; the town adjacent to us is a pretty affluent community.

One night, we got a Twelve Step call from a man... [whom] I knew somewhat. He was a real "captain of industry" in an international corporation. He was really a "big bucks" guy! I knew from the address that he lived in a neighborhood called Millionaire's Row. We went over there; I took a new guy with me. When we rang the bell, the guy came to the door in a smoking jacket. I had never seen one in real life, only in the movies. He had his music system going; "Old Blue Eyes" was singing. He said, "Want me to turn it off?" I replied, "Nah, let it finish the song — I like that guy."

He said, "Would you like me to tell you about myself?" And I said, "That would be interesting, why don't you do that." So he began to talk, and eventually he said, "This is not the first time that I've tried to get sober. I've done a lot of stuff. I've talked to everybody in the United States and other countries who think they know anything about alcoholism. Every expert I can possibly conceive of. I've been in every kind of treatment center that you can imagine.

"I just got out of one that ripped me off for thirty thousand dollars." I said, "Well that's pretty expensive," and I let him continue. He followed by saying, "The last person… [who] made a call on me like you guys are doing ripped me off for thirty thousand dollars." He took a deep breath and said, "Now what do you suppose you can tell me that I don't already know?"

And I said, "Well, probably nothing. But there is one thing that I want you to know. Be sure to understand that this fellow and I wouldn't sell you thirty minutes of our time doing what we're doing for thirty thousand dollars, because you just can't buy it!" That old boy melted. He

absolutely melted, and he never had another drink. He
stayed sober for eleven years and died sober.

What I'm talking about is, when you get the money,
the property, and the prestige and allow these things to
overshadow what your recovery is about, you pay for
it. You pay for it with your life! So it's a very important
Tradition.[5]

Each member certainly may have a slightly different
take on this Tradition, and that is encouraged, of course.
Nevertheless, the Sixth Tradition is designed to remind
the groups that they need to guard themselves from
these temptations.

At the 1950 Cleveland Convention, Gene from
Toledo explained the Sixth Tradition this way:

12 "An A.A. group ought never endorse, finance, or lend the
A.A. name to any related facility or outside enterprise, lest
problems of money, property, and prestige divert us from
our primary spiritual aim."

Well, there again, I think of those green pastures that
are so tempting. What are these diversionary activities?
Well, I can mention a few of them, which are obvious.
One would be hospitals, for instance; clubs, drying-out
places, educational enterprises, literature, and perhaps the
authorship of literature. All of these things again may be
offshoots of the growth of knowledge and the eagerness for
public information about this problem with which we deal.

I can recall in our own community, seven years ago we
had no facilities whatever for hospitalization. Rarely, some

individual might be taken to a general hospital because his doctor was on the staff there and had an "in." But for the ordinary, run-of-mine drunk, there was just no place to take him except into our homes. And I remember in one stage of our development, one of our members had a friend who was manager of a fairly good hotel in Toledo. And they were very generous with us and we at one time, we had as many as four and five patients at a time in rooms at the hotel. And we AAs were alternating our shifts to help these drunks get sober. They said that when you walked into the lobby of the Willard you could smell the paraldehyde.

That went on for a little while. Until all of a sudden it seemed like the Lord sent us a great benefactor. Sometimes in AA, I think we almost become superstitious about what Providence will do for us. But that's another story. I think Providence has been with us since the beginning of time.

It took a long, long time, but there's no question in my mind about the divine origin of Alcoholics Anonymous. But this man, as I say, seemed to have been sent from heaven. He was a drunk and he was a man of means and rather high standing in the community. In a recent business transaction, he had acquired a building for which he had no current use. He came into AA, and I can remember hearing him in his second or third meeting. He just caught fire. He picked up the book and said, "Why, I could have written that book." Well, might he have, but he didn't. I remember another peculiarity about him. You know, we always harped on the first drink, but he said it wasn't the first one. It was the second one. That was the bad one for him, the second one.

He proposed that he would set up a hospital in the unoccupied building that was now under his ownership. And we in our group were about to undertake that; we were going to run the hospital. As far as I know, there may be a number of groups that do conduct some kind of hospital facility. But I'm telling you, the only thing that saved us from what would have been a colossal error was the hand of Providence. Number one, our great philanthropist didn't get along very well with this program; I guess it was that second drink. Number two, he passed to another life the following summer; I think this was a period of five or six months. So we didn't get our hospital.

The point is, at that time I would have eagerly gone for a hospital that would have been run by our group. Suppose we had gotten into it at that time. Here our poor, misguided friend missed the boat, and then up and dies on us, and leaves us with his estate to deal with. An alcoholics' hospital running and a piece of property that has to be liquidated. It is, as Dick has said. "Tradition is something like everything else we've got in AA. It seems like it has to be the hard way. We got it through trial and error, and the things that are suggested here today are things that are suggested for the greater good of all.

As a lawyer, I can assure you that the substance of our activity, the spiritual content of it, is in our Twelve Steps and in our carrying those Twelve Steps to other alcoholics. But in corporate activity, and I mean by that any form or ramification of business activity, anything that involves money, does seem to be the better part of wisdom. We are not alone in the experience of Alcoholics Anonymous, but I can assure that from the standpoint of a lawyer, that we should let those enterprises stand on their own feet detached, segregated, separated from AA.

There are a lot of good things that can be done in the field of alcoholism. Many are in hearty accord, but most of them we shouldn't touch. We may cooperate, we may sustain by our cooperation, but it would be much better if we didn't try to manage, in my humble opinion. Let us be devoted to the real purpose of Alcoholics Anonymous, the real purpose of our home groups, and my real purpose and yours in life. There has been entrusted to us a tremendously powerful message for human good. Let us be singly, unitedly devoted to carrying that message.[6]

Some people believe that after seventy-five years of success AA shouldn't worry about the idea of affiliating with anyone. They claim AA is strong enough to withstand any potential fallout brought about by a relationship with an outside entity. Perhaps their claim is accurate that AA as a whole is strong enough to handle these types of relationships, but is the individual member?

Once members are lured into the illusion that capitalizing on the AA name for their own personal benefit is acceptable, they may begin to isolate themselves from other members. This disassociation and lack of unity often leads the alcoholic into trouble. Clearly, cooperation and not affiliation will guide AA successfully forward.

7
Paying Our Own Way

*I*n 1948, when $10,000 would buy a good house or six new cars, a certain woman died after willing that amount to Alcoholics Anonymous. Bill W., who was strapped for cash most of the time, admitted that AA could use such a gift for service functions.

However, it was declined on the basis of the newly formed Tradition Seven, which stated: "Every A.A. group ought to be fully self-supporting, declining outside contributions."[1] Declining a gift in this amount was such an unusual action that the story even made it to newspapers throughout the country.

Why did AA develop such a tradition? Like any organization, AA needed money for various operations. Money was needed to pay for meeting locations, coffee, literature, and other items. The service offices needed support. So how and why exactly did AA get so high and mighty that it could turn down such a sizable gift that was made in good faith?

Bill W., as usual, had a good answer. In many of his speeches he discussed the activities of AA's early days and referenced the above-mentioned bequest. He acknowledged that previous outside contributions, in many cases from nonalcoholics, had made the Alcoholic Foundation Office (later named the General Service Office or GSO) possible. He even credited Charlie Towns and John D. Rockefeller with providing money that made the publishing of the book *Alcoholics Anonymous* possible. These outside contributions also provided a small weekly stipend for him and Dr. Bob to draw from while AA was getting off the ground. Understandably, AA owes a tremendous debt of gratitude to these early outside contributors.

But as AA grew and became self-supporting, Bill and the other founders insisted that AA pay its own way. By the late 1940s, AA members' combined yearly earnings was likely in the millions. It was clear that AA needed no financial help from anyone outside of the fellowship. And if the general public wanted to help, there were plenty of other organizations and educational institutions that were dealing with research and professional training in the field of alcoholism. Their money could be used to support one of these other efforts.

Of course AA toed the line of not having *any opinion* on what any of these contributors or organizations chose to do—the only insistence was that the AA name be kept out of it. The philosophy was that too much money would harm AA and possibly compromise the simple spiritual principles that were helping so many people stay sober. The membership learned that they ought to be givers and not takers, thereby focusing on the principle of service — *for fun and for free.*

There were other good reasons for declining outside contributions, one of the more obvious being that financial support risked the possibility that outside donors might want to exercise a measure of control. Any organization or association that depends on donated funds usually pays special attention to the views of those who supply the funds, and can withdraw them at any time. Since AA needed to be free from any duty, except the primary purpose of carrying the recovery message to those who still suffer, it could not be involved in other purposes.

In a 2001 interview, AA member Howard P. told the following story. It dramatically illustrates the temptation to take money when it's offered to an AA group, especially for alcoholics who have been programmed to believe that financial gain equals success.

> I once watched a movie on training wild elephants in India. The training starts for the baby elephants when the trainer ties a rope around the baby elephant's right front leg and ties the other end of the rope to a large tree. The baby elephant had always been allowed to run free with the herd, but now he is held tight to the tree by the rope. It pulls and tugs against the rope but is held tight; and after a while it comes to believe that when the rope is tight it is futile to pull. After that it just stands there, defeated.

The trainer then goes on with the rest of its training, always reinforcing the truth that when the rope is tight on its right leg it is futile to pull. At the end of the movie a huge elephant is shown with a large tree trunk secured to its harness and it pulls that tree out of the forest for harvest. At the lunch break, in order to hold the big elephant where they want it, they drive a relatively short stake deep enough into the ground; that when they tie one end of rope around the big elephant's leg and the other end around the stake, the rope will get tight when the elephant reaches the end of the rope and he will not pull against the tight rope. The truth is that the stake does not hold the elephant; the rope does not hold the elephant. It is the limiting belief that was imposed on him when he was a baby that holds the elephant. Once a baby elephant learns a "truth" and that truth is properly reinforced, it will always remain "the truth"; whether it is actually true or not.

That same process applies to human beings as well as it applies to elephants. When I was a baby elephant my culture taught me that I was separate from God; with God up in heaven behind the pearly gates on the streets of gold, while I was down here on earth, separate from God. My culture further taught me that I should be an individual achiever who could win the competition with others so that I would be the best or the boss. That being the best or the boss puts me in a position to gain money, prestige, and authority; and on that basis, for me to secure a sense of well-being. The ideas that "quitters never win and winners never quit," "you put your shoulder to the wheel" and "your nose to the grindstone," "the devil will take the hindmost," and the story about the "little engine that could" all became powerful motivational "baby elephant beliefs" in my young life. These baby elephant beliefs certainly served as bedrock on which I built the insane … delusion that I could wrest satisfaction and happiness out of this world if I only managed well.

It also turns out that the human central nervous system includes neurotransmitters called *norepineph-rine*, which activate the fight or flight centers in the brain to help provide the motivation to win the competition. Other neurotransmitters called *dopamine* and *serotonin* activate the pleasure centers in the brain to generate the sense of well-being promised for winning the competition. Today, science tells us that alcoholics and addicts are in the top fifty percent of the population in terms of the abundance of norepinephrine and in the bottom fifty percent in terms of the abundance of dopamine and serotonin. Therefore, these people as a group are spring-loaded to win the competition but seldom experience the ongoing sense of well-being promised by their culture because they have those biochemical imbalances in their central nervous systems.

Many times we think of that sense of well-being as feeling normal. This past weekend, I heard a speaker talk about it at the Florida State Convention. She said, "When I had my first drink, I knew what it was like to feel normal." She said it three times. She knew what it was like to feel normal. Well, that's not right. We feel two, or even three times better than normal, and the brain becomes addicted to that feeling, because it has never felt normally good.

Normal, at least in terms of what our culture has imposed on us. Because we become addicted, we ultimately end up pitifully and incomprehensibly demoralized.

I went into AA, and nearly everything that I had learned about what was the right thing to do for me was wrong. Surrender. Well, surrender isn't included in the competition. You see, when competing with everybody, the winners never quit. And the quitters never win. Those are clichés that come to us from our culture. And we need money. By my first few weeks in AA, I had picked my home group — the Culver City California Studio group. This group met in the Culver City Women's Club, where it had for twenty-five years. That facility was purchased by the Sons of Norway, who told us we were going to have to move our Friday night meeting, because they wanted their meetings on Friday night and they owned the building.

I told Frank, "You mean you've been paying rent for twenty-five years? If you had just bought the building you would have been paying a mortgage and you would own the building instead of the Sons of Norway. What the hell is the matter with AA, that they don't buy their own building?" Frank's explanation was that owning property isn't a productive thing for Alcoholics Anonymous to stay in unity. Without having fights, owning property invariably ends up in battle. So the Traditions keep us from doing those things.

I was thinking about how I could promote through fund-raising money to come into AA. It seemed like all the good ideas that I had held all my life and the things I had become good at were at a time I was drinking and using successfully. I had become good at this, and now that I was sober, I could do this goodness for AA. It seems like every one of my best ideas, Frank would point out a Tradition; we read them every meeting, and I listened to an extent. To me, it was just a series of speed bumps and old-fashioned ideas that made no sense at all. Not when we look at the real problem and we are looking for real solutions. Frank was about the only guy I could talk to about this, but still we mostly just focused on the Steps.

I was a year sober when I became the Central Service Representative for a ... group. I then became there what is the zone delegate for the Central Service meeting. I also became the treasurer. We had a representative from the courts, a lawyer, come to us and say: "(Someone) had first come to Central Office (to schedule a business meeting of some sort) and Central Office said that needs to be presented to the Central Service Committee."

The presentation was that we had just inherited eighty-seven thousand dollars, but this time I somehow knew that we hadn't inherited anything. I knew we were not going to accept this. We hadn't discussed it between us in any way. There was a lady from Inglewood, California, who was constantly picking on me about my not adhering to the Traditions the same way she did. She was the chairman of the committee. She responded to the guy by saying, "Traditionally, Alcoholics Anonymous does not accept money from any outside sources. We support ourselves and if we can't support ourselves then we will stop existing. But we will not accept any money from any outside sources."

I knew that she was right, and as the treasurer, I knew that at that particular time of the year we were in the red. We had a prudent reserve to cover our bills, but the Central Office Executive Director showed me that historically during that period of time, we didn't have enough income to cover our current expense. He said, "We have enough savings, we have a prudent reserve from which we always take a dip. But in the long run, we add to the prudent reserve, up to a particular point." I had gone through that with him, and could see that was true. So although we were in the red, we did not need that eighty-seven thousand dollars.

The lawyer said, "Well whether you accept it or not, the court will want to know what you want done with the money." And the little lady, that little old lady from Inglewood said, "Oh, we have another Tradition that we have no interest in outside issues. We have no opinion; we have no recommendation to the court at all. We are not involved in this and you cannot involve us."

And I knew I felt the power of that, and I'm sure everybody else did. We had a newcomer guy who wasn't part of the committee; however, the membership was always welcome to the committee, and he asked if he could participate. He proposed a way of having the court distribute the money to individual groups and then to have the groups submit it. The little lady told him, "We appreciate what your idea is and how you're trying to help AA, but I want you to know that we are the Central Service Committee for AA in Los Angeles, and we don't look for ways to circumvent the Traditions. We look for ways of conforming to the Traditions." [2]

There is also the risk of accumulating funds above and beyond the modest needs of the group. Acquiring a substantial contribution could build up a group's bank balance, much higher than an ordinary prudent reserve would be. This could be an easy target for misuse, or become an issue causing dissension and ill will in the group. It often takes very little money to start a fight over how it should be spent.

It might have been in AA's good fortune that the fellowship was launched in the middle of the Depression in the 1930s. Virtually every candidate for AA membership was flat broke, not only because of alcoholism but also because times were very bad. When Bill W. made the call that finally led him to Dr. Bob, he had just gone through a business setback and had less than ten dollars. He was also facing an unpaid hotel bill. When the early members met, they could barely afford coffee and doughnuts. Dr. Bob faced the likelihood of losing his house, and Bill's own residence in New York was eventually taken over by the mortgage holder. Newcomers to AA needed financial help, but nobody was able to give it.

What this taught them was that money had nothing to do with getting sober and helping others. The members' real assets were their own stories and their ability to share experiences, strength, and hope. It worked, and AA was born and thrived.

There is also something to be said for the bitter experiences that Bill W. had gone through in his own work on Wall Street. He had started his business career with a fierce ambition, a desire to be Number One. But his alcoholism, and a few bad breaks, landed him on the rocks. He saw his ambition may have been a component of his problem. And fortunately, it was easy to see that it took very little money to provide the resources that AA groups needed.

At the same time, Bill and the AA pioneers took justifiable pride in the fact that sobriety also helped members become employable and responsible. Just as members were able to become self-supporting through the program, it became important for AA to also become self-supporting.

The speaker selected to share on this Tradition at the 1950 International Convention was Fred from Florida:

🜹 Mr. Chairman and friends, Tradition number Seven:
13 "Every AA group ought to be fully self-supporting, declining outside contributions." I dare say that in the early days of AA, that was very easily understood because as small groups we met in homes. And money was beside the point. [As] we began to grow, we looked for larger quarters and the question of a little light bill and a little rent became involved. We were not too particular about the passing of the hat at these little home meetings, but when these other things came up, we had to sit up and take a little notice. And of course you know, the Tradition tells us that in the passing of the hat, we all remember one thing that we learned or tried to learn very early in AA, and that is our honesty. I believe as a matter of record, we have not lost the hat.

Now a little early enthusiasm went [where] money [was] involved. Some of us will say, those who might have been a little bit more fortunate than others were throwing those dollars bills in once or twice a week, sometimes three times a week. All according to what our ambition was. Then we began to do a little figuring: two and two made four, four and four made eight. Eight bucks is a lot of money, and we [decide that we] have got to cut that down. So we back it in [half dollars] and then into [quarters], and the next thing you know ... we would go all the way to nickels and dimes. Then when the lights and rent were due, we were running a little short.

Along with that, people were becoming more interested in our work. The first thing they asked was, "How can I help? What can I give you?" We said, "Very sorry, but we don't accept any outside donations." We grew and we grew and the public became more and more interested. Some people were very much interested in our work and decided that it would be a fine gesture to make larger offers that we would go for. I'd say just recently, it was last year sometime, that in Miami we had an offer of twenty-five thousand dollars. That's a lot of money. A lot of fears went up. We were straining at the Traditions, but fortunately there were enough among [us] who had read and understood the Traditions. We remembered being told that in the early days, one of the greatest mistakes that could be made was for Alcoholics Anonymous to accept a large amount of money. So the consensus of opinion was "no" on the twenty-five thousand dollars.[3]

Is it right to say that AA groups are fully self-supporting when they use church facilities and other meeting rooms, sometimes at reduced rates? This is something that individual groups must work out when they seek accommodations for meetings. Most AA groups undoubtedly pay going rates for the facilities they use, and they must also demonstrate the ability to keep the meeting rooms in good order. This is also part of being self-supporting.

Recently, I was talking with a woman at an AA convention and she told me this interesting story about a group she belonged to and the Seventh Tradition:

> One night at the meeting we went around the room and introduced ourselves, as is the custom in our group. Now, this was a closed meeting. A man introduced himself as Dave, an alcoholic. The lady next to him said, "I'm here to support Dave." The meeting chairperson interrupted and explained that a "closed" meeting was for alcoholics only. She was not welcome at a closed meeting, but would be welcome to attend any "open" meetings. Both she and her husband got up and left.
>
> A few days later, one of the members who was instrumental in arranging the meeting place with the church received a phone call. It was from the head pastor, who was very concerned about this issue. Apparently Dave and his wife were very important members of the church, and happened to be the church's largest financial contributors. He was very concerned that this couple was not welcome at AA, and wanted the rule changed.

The AA member, who had a very good understanding of the Traditions, was able to explain to the minister that the AA group pays ... [its] rent every month. The group is self-supporting, and is in no way associated with the church, other than as a tenant. She went on to explain that this was one reason that each AA group paid ... [its] own way, so that the possibility of pressures from outside of AA would be eliminated. She also explained the Tradition of nonaffiliation, concluding the conversation by offering to have one of the members take Dave and his wife to an open meeting. The situation worked out fine and the group continues to meet in the church.[4]

AA meetings are also held in treatment centers and public institutions, such as prisons. As a general rule, the treatment center meetings are just that, meetings, not therapy groups. Most prisons have their own AA groups that conform to the AA Traditions and are entitled to be listed as groups within the General Service structure.

In recent years, some government-sponsored efforts devoted to the addiction treatment and recovery field have stipulated that there should be no mention of God or a Higher Power in the various programs being offered. This demonstrates the type of control that programs being supported by sources outside of AA might come under. Whether we agree with such requirements or not, any AA group should be entirely free to follow its own course in working with alcoholics. If the group is fully self-supporting, as Tradition Seven suggests, the group will be free to conduct its business in the way that best serves the group. AA's overall principle of giving freely is that which has been freely given.

Tradition Seven also seems to be compatible with the general belief that alcoholics are difficult to manage and dislike being controlled by others. This might not be entirely true, but most AA members have probably seen traces of that independent streak in their own groups. Since groups sometimes have difficulty getting their own members to go along with any direction, things would probably be even worse if the direction came from outside the group. Members ought to be grateful that Tradition Seven was adopted, especially when the basket is passed!

8

Freely Ye
Have Received,
Freely Give

*I*t is rarely mentioned, but one factor that gives AA great leverage with newcomers is that nobody gets paid for carrying the message. The meter is never running, and nobody gets a bill for services rendered. In fact, the person receiving the message is even assured that the messengers protect their own sobriety by helping others.

It is also understood that the person carrying the message has no special expertise other than personal experience in the program. The recovered alcoholic, in effect, is on the same level as the person needing help; no diplomas or academic courses are needed to carry the AA message. This is not likely to change, because the idea of "freely carrying the message" is enshrined in Tradition Eight:

> *Alcoholics Anonymous should remain forever nonpro-*
> *fessional, but our service centers may employ special*
> *workers.*[1]

However, this Tradition did not become fully understood and accepted without considerable argument and discussion over the years. In *Twelve Steps and Twelve Traditions*, Bill W. stated emphatically that

> *Alcoholics simply will not listen to a paid twelfth-stepper. Almost from the beginning, we have been positive that face-to-face work with the alcoholic who suffers could be based only on the desire to help and be helped. When an A.A. talks for money, whether at a meeting or to a single newcomer, it can have a very bad effect on him, too. The money motive compromises him and everything he says and does for his prospect. This has always been so obvious that only a very few A.A.s have ever worked the Twelfth Step for a fee.[2]*

Since Bill provided no examples of Twelfth Steppers who actually attempted to charge fees, we have no further information regarding the outcomes of such actions. We can understand how the relationship between sponsor and sponsee would change if fees were part of the equation. For one thing, the sponsor would then likely be held accountable for a successful outcome that he could not really guarantee. We would no longer just be carrying the message. We might also be subject to governmental rules and regulations that don't exist under our present system. And, to add a facetious but serious note, we would have to face the fact that many alcoholics have trouble paying their bills.

Bill W. shared his views at the Cleveland International Convention:

14 Tradition number Eight: "Alcoholics Anonymous should remain forever nonprofessional, but our service centers may employ special workers." This has been given a lot of room for thought, questions, and, in some cases, arguments. Like a great many other things, we have been able to iron out the wrinkles, and along with being more or less schooled in the development of understanding, we arrived at certain things, whereby today I don't believe we have too much trouble. From time to time, and we're never going to please them all, we do hear a few grunts and groans and gripes about the man or woman who has a job in AA... There's a job to be filled, a job that will take time and effort, and a job that you would have to pay someone for; this, and this is another consensus of opinion over a period of years, the alcoholic or the member of A.A. who is qualified we feel is justified to take that job. And we feel justified in paying them. As a young secretary in my early A.A. days, I was exposed to something a little bit new and different every once in a while. I had the novel experience, you might call it, of being offered two thousand dollars for saving a member of a family. Two uncles and a brother pleaded with me to "take this money and take over this boy so that we can straighten him out." Now you know there was a little element of temptation there, but I had to say no. It's a good thing for me that I did. It's a good thing for anybody who might be exposed to temptations of this kind to just take some time to think. A thought doesn't take more than a few seconds, and if you understand it as I did at that time, your answer too would be no.

In reference to the jobs mentioned, from this time in Cleveland [the members who were critical of hiring an AA member as a professional administrator] need bear in mind the enormity of this job; the responsibility of it. If it falls on one man, who has given up considerable amounts of his time, many weeks in advance of this convention; to handle it properly it is a full-time commitment. There are professionals with experience in this line of work, but they require a high salary. So they took it upon themselves to put this man in his job and to pay him.

I have talked to a great many people, and in my opinion, this man should not be criticized for taking money for the job he did. We pay only those ... [who] can do the work that is so necessary in the growing up of our organization.[3]

It is a fact that today, a number of recovered alcoholics in AA also serve as counselors or have another professional connection that is related to addiction treatment and recovery. Early AA members used the term *two hatters* to describe such persons. Wearing one hat, the individual attends AA meetings and sponsors others. Wearing a second hat, the person goes to work as a counselor or therapist and carries on the work in the same manner as others would in the same field.

AA member Tom I. shared some of his experience with this Tradition:

Eight has to do with "not selling what we give away."
There were talks of Bill getting involved in working with
hospitals, including discussions about possible chains of
hospitals [in AA's early days]. This is, in part, what gen-
erated the need for the Eighth Tradition. AA itself needs
always remain nonprofessional because you can't sell a
spiritual gift. That is what we have—a spiritual gift. We
are not selling a product—that's not what we're about.
The whole experience of the program where Bill met with
Bob and Bob stressed how important it was that he and
Bill talked about their experience, not knowledge. This is
the bonding that occurs, and is what we need to preserve.

If we follow that principle, we won't be "hustling" in
AA—we are not going to be selling to people. Not everybody practices this, however, not by any means. There
are people who sell their service, but unfortunately in the
process, also sell their souls. This is something that cannot
happen.

When I first got into the program, this Tradition was
extremely helpful to me in several ways. When I was
first employed to work in a prison system, I didn't really
have any old greybeards to talk with about it. Nobody had
dealt with this sort of thing before. So this Tradition was
extremely important to me. Tradition Eight and a couple
others were extremely important in keeping proper balance in what I was doing, especially considering that I had
just been paroled from a maximum custody penitentiary
about two years earlier. Then, there I was, employed as a
professional employee in a corrections system, with a lot of
my work being done in a maximum custody penitentiary.

That was heady wine. I had to do a lot of thinking — just me and my Higher Power having these conversations, because nobody else could talk about personal experience.

My sponsor was able to offer some insights and understanding, but he had never stood where I was. I became centered on this Tradition, because if I was going to wear the title of a prison official, then that is what I would be. I was not going to try and work both sides of the street. I could have been a real hoodlum hero, the toast of the world's prison population, on the cover of every tabloid in the world. That would have been unbelievable!

What I had to resolve was that I was not for sale. I respect anonymity, and I also respect that a gift is to be given. So I made up my mind when I began my professional career that I would not become some kind of hoodlum hero. I was going to take my place in the agency and do my job. If I was paid for a job, I was going to be a professional employee. Practicing these principles in my professional career for thirty-nine years led me to the top of my profession until my retirement.

The thing that I notice with people and their sponsors is that for anyone who goes into the field of alcoholic treatment, there's a sharp distinction between what you sell as a professional and what you give away. I don't care if you're an aide or an orderly who works in a treatment center, you do your job, and you're not a professional AA. If I am working with someone who is working in a setting like that, when I talk to them, I'm not only participating in their life, but I'm watching them. What I'm looking for is somebody sitting in a discussion meeting who is counseling, rather than sharing. When I see that, he and I will go to the woodshed; same if a guy is speaking at a meeting. If he starts making what sounds like a treatment lecture, there will be another trip involved. That is exactly what gets you into trouble, when you start marketing a spiritual gift. That cannot be done, and should be called prostitution.

I received a call one day from a lady I've known for many years. She had been a solid AA member for years, a Ph.D., and a very sharp woman. I knew she was working with the mental health system somewhere. She told me that she would buy me lunch…so I said, "Okay, I'll go."

She was troubled.…She said, "Tom, you're still active in AA, aren't you?" I said, "Yes, aren't you?" She replied by saying, "No." So I inquired, "Well that's too bad, why not?" It was a sad thing she said: "I gave at the office."

That is what happens when you get distorted about your God-given gift and you try to sell it to somebody else. My God, that's an untenable position. To me that's what is so important about this — we cannot sell this gift. I can give you hundreds of stories about that. But that's exactly what it comes down to: "I gave at the office." That is a sad, sad culmination of a very bright woman. She had been in AA for twenty years.

We have many people who get into trouble thinking that a sales job they have given to themselves is a form of recovery. When that paycheck hits, it is pretty hard to reconcile that as a gift. I think it's important for sponsors to help folks to hang on to that principle. You can't sell it. You have to give it away — otherwise it doesn't count.[4]

Sometimes, Tradition Eight can be misunderstood. Mel B. remembers such a case from many years ago. His first sponsor, Maury, was an orderly in the state hospital where Mel landed as an alcoholic patient. At that time, hospital orderlies at that particular institution were at the very bottom of the pay scale. Maury and his wife, who was also an orderly, earned barely enough between the two of them to afford a modest apartment and put their two teenaged daughters through school. Their car had a few dents and rattles.

Maury, as a devoted AA member, helped to persuade the hospital administration to allow AA meetings in the hospital's main building. One stipulation was that an orderly was required to be in attendance. Maury was assigned the job of collecting the patients, taking them to the meetings, and making sure they returned to their respective wards.

Some members in the local community raised objections, feeling that Maury was being paid to carry the AA message! Actually, he was only being paid to serve as an orderly and comply with the hospital's rules. Any orderly could have carried out the same duties. The furor soon passed, and Maury continued in his work; but he was somewhat hurt by the misunderstanding about Tradition Eight.

The positive aspect of this misunderstanding was that members, even in 1950, were conscientious about following the letter of Tradition Eight. This Tradition has now become so engrained in AA practice that it would be almost unthinkable for anyone to professionalize the program.

The second part of Tradition Eight notes that our service centers may employ special workers. Even this brought contention in AA, though it was obvious that the fellowship had certain needs that required paid employees. Volunteers performed service functions for a short time, but it was not practical on a long-term basis. These service functions were not Twelfth Step work, but as Bill pointed out, they did make Twelfth Step work possible.

In most cities, it is necessary to have a central office that is staffed by one or more persons who handle the clerical functions and answer the telephone. While volunteers often help, a more reliable practice is to have paid personnel who keep regular hours in the office. If they are also AA members, they are not being paid to carry the AA message; they are being paid to make Twelfth Step work possible, as Bill noted. The office also has other expenses that have to be met. All of these costs have to be paid by the AA community, in line with our Tradition of being self-supporting.

Members can be grateful for the examples set by the pioneering members. In its very beginnings, AA had no literature, and its General Service Office (GSO) consisted of Bill W. and one nonalcoholic secretary, Ruth Hock. The office really was the surviving facility of a failed business venture that Bill had shared with Hank P., an early member who gave an outstanding service by getting the Big Book published in 1939. At first, they viewed the book as a money-making venture. It did provide some revenue, as they struggled to keep the office open. In time, the trustees also voted to grant Big Book royalties to Bill W. and Dr. Bob.

This action, however, brought initial opposition from a few Cleveland members. Bill W. was able to present audited information about GSO operations, which helped settle the matter, and brought a full endorsement of GSO's work from the Cleveland Central Committee. The incident did underscore the need to keep groups fully informed. Since 1955, GSO operations have been linked to the General Service Conference.

Over the many years since the Twelve Traditions were formally adopted, there has been a general acceptance of the idea that Twelfth Step work should be freely given, while other work can be handled on a paid basis. All of the employees at the GSO are paid salaries reasonably equivalent to what they would earn elsewhere. Though it is located in New York City, this office is not the contact point for alcoholics seeking help. There is a New York intergroup office for that purpose.

Bill W. was the one person who served at GSO in later years without a salary. His income came from royalties from the Big Book, as well as other writings. This too brought criticism, and the practice today is for GSO to pay writers and artists, as well as other professionals who produce conference-approved literature on a work-for-hire basis. The rule within the spirit of the Tradition is clear — if AA would have to pay someone to provide a needed service, such as

Central Office manager, accountant, janitor, and so on, and a member is hired to do the work, then he or she should be compensated for the work.

The last fifty years have been challenging for many AA members because understanding and conforming to this Tradition can be somewhat confusing. The need for professionals in the field of addiction and education has steadily increased. Many of these positions are filled by people who have found sobriety through AA and other Twelve Step programs. They have then gone on to take the necessary classes for certification in their field so that they can be employed as a professional.

As with all other outside issues, AA, as an organization, has no opinion on what the individual member does for a livelihood or vocation. The Tradition simply suggests that no one be paid for AA Twelve Step work — members should not advertise themselves as AA counselors, or anything else that is AA related. AA simply has members, and each member is exactly the same as every other member. The best guide is for each member to decide on the direction that is best for him or her. If a person feels that his or her work is too close to Twelve Step work, then that person might choose another profession. Common sense and the advice of a good sponsor will help direct those who might stumble on the issue of what constitutes mixing professionalism with AA.

Some AA members confuse this Tradition and believe that any member who draws an income from any source related to the recovery field is in some way violating the Tradition or taking advantage of AA. Nothing could be further from the truth. Bill W. was very clear when discussing the principle of Tradition Eight, and most people understand that as long as they don't charge for Twelve Step Work, "carrying the message" to the next alcoholic, one alcoholic to another, they have conformed to Tradition Eight.

9
An Anarchy
That Works

One bit of AA lore speakers like to share is that Bill W. really wanted to set the fellowship running similarly to that of a franchise and that he was restrained by Dr. Bob. While this seems to fit the image of Bill as a hard-driving businessman, the truth is, Bill realized from the beginning that for AA to work, it couldn't function like a commercial business venture. Bill actually saw AA as a sort of an anarchy that would work as long as members continued to follow its principles. Bill wrote in Tradition Nine: "A.A., as such, ought never be organized; but we may create service boards or committees directly responsible to those they serve."[1]

A first thought about this Tradition is that it was directly opposite to Bill's early ambitions. In his personal story in the book *Alcoholics Anonymous* Bill revealed that he returned from World War I service in the army with the belief that he would head an organization. He wrote, "My talent for leadership, I imagined, would place me at the head of vast enterprises which I would manage with the utmost assurance."[2]

Bill's drinking eliminated any chance for such success, although he did display an ability to round up the investors who went broke with him in 1929. But once he found sobriety, he soon had an opportunity to join a proxy fight for control of a troubled machine-tool company in Akron, Ohio. He looked forward to reorganizing the company as its new president. He undoubtedly knew just what steps he would take to make the business profitable again. Once the proxy battle was finished, he would spend all his time shaping up the new organization. Helping another alcoholic would have been at the bottom of his to-do list.

As we know today, things didn't work out that way. Bill lost the proxy battle, but found a new mission that led to the founding of AA. In its own way, AA then became a vast enterprise, although much different from the businesses Bill wanted to run. He did become AA's pioneering leader, but only as a trusted servant; in 1955, he graciously turned over the service responsibility to the General Service Conference.

But what if Bill and the other AA pioneers had decided to organize AA the same way that corporations and various other associations are set up? As a broker, he would have issued stock, or had membership fees. There would certainly have been a president, numerous vice presidents, as well as a cluster of managers. The organization would have a number of levels with certain individuals having more power and prestige than others. There would also have been frequent elections to frame policies and make way for management changes. It is likely that the organization would go through countless power struggles and arguments about the best ways to deliver services to the still-suffering alcoholic. Along the way, most of AA's basic principles might have been altered just to meet the needs of the organization.

AA is often referred to as a simple program, and it's easy to see that, contrary to the corporate scenario we've described, its governance can be very simple. Since the main work of AA rests within the groups and individual members, all that's needed is a service office to provide literature and helpful advice while representing the program to the public. The General Service Office in New York can provide helpful assistance and suggestions, but it has no authority over the groups and cannot issue orders. This is also true at the local level; having people available to answer the telephone and handle literature and correspondence is usually all that is needed.

Where businesses or associations generally have a power structure with an authoritative figure in charge, AA's General Service Office leads only by suggestion, even on matters that are vital to its own interests.

Mel B. recalls an incident that reflects this kind of leadership. Some years ago, he was contacted by the PBS show *History Detectives* to discuss a letter of condolence that Bill W. had written in the early 1940s. Mel was to be interviewed for the show in front of Bill and Lois's former home at 182 Clinton Street in Brooklyn.

Would this be a violation of personal anonymity? He telephoned GSO for an answer.

Mel was given prompt assurance that there was no violation as long as he did not identify himself as an AA member. Like any person, he was free to talk about Bill and AA to anybody. The staff member who discussed it with him didn't even offer an opinion about the advisability of appearing on the show. Mel accepted the invitation. The show went smoothly and appeared to present both Bill W. and AA in a positive way.

How did AA arrive at its decision not to be organized? Most of the credit for this development certainly goes to Bill W., as is demonstrated in his writings and discussions. Bill realized that he and Dr. Bob had become the de facto leaders of AA, simply because they were the founders. Their power and influence had derived from the gratitude of the members who followed them. There was a general belief that they had the necessary wisdom and humility to guide the fellowship. None of the other AA pioneers could possibly maintain the same stature as the two founders. But who would provide leadership after they were gone?

This Tradition was introduced by the speaker at the Cleveland Convention, George from Carlsbad, California. Here is what this pioneer had to say:

> 15 I have been given the assignment of Traditions Nine and Ten. And I shall not presume upon your intelligence with any lengthy discussion. In fact, I feel like Jonah did when the whale swallowed him. The whale said, "Jonah, I feel

sick to my stomach." And Jonah said, "We'd both be a hell of a better sight if you'd kept your big mouth shut."

I will read Tradition Nine: "AA, as such, ought never be organized, but we may create service boards or committees directly responsible to those they serve." Now in my opinion and from my experience in different groups...I have found that there was a tendency for the "greybeards" to take charge. In my own case, I came into AA in a very large area — in a large city group — and afterwards I moved to a smaller group. And I hadn't yet learned that I had not filed down my ego sufficiently, so I undertook the carriage of this small group of Alcoholics Anonymous. [I had] the city slicker's idea that they were so-so and my way was better....

Today I wish to say, gratefully, through Divine Providence, that a little of my ego has filed itself down to the point...where now I realize that each group is its own. It elects its officers and controls itself. [The group] at all times remembers that we are all united for our common welfare, and each person's recovery depends upon it. Within all these Traditions, it is a fact that they (work together, each supporting the others), like our Twelve Steps.[3]

The long form of Tradition Nine reads:

Each A.A. group needs the least possible organization. Rotating leadership is the best. The small group may elect its secretary, the large group its rotating committee, and the groups of a large metropolitan area their central or intergroup committee, which often employs a full-time secretary. The trustees of the General Service Board are, in effect, our A.A. General Service Committee. They are the custodians of our A.A. Tradition and the receivers of voluntary A.A. contributions by which we maintain our A.A. General Service Office at New York. They are authorized by the groups to handle our overall public relations and they guarantee the integrity of our principal newspaper, the A.A. Grapevine. All such representatives are to be guided in the spirit of service, for true leaders in A.A. are but trusted and experienced servants of the whole. They derive no real authority from their titles; they do not govern. Universal respect is the key to their usefulness.[4]

There was also the unfortunate example of the Oxford Group, which had supplied many of AA's spiritual principles. In the early years of the organization its founder, Frank Buchman, was a man of great personal integrity and spirituality. But as time went on, many thought that he also had a tendency to control his followers beyond what was needed. After a serious public relations blunder in 1936 with some careless remarks about Hitler, he refused to admit his mistake or take any steps to repair the damage. This hampered the Oxford Group's ability to attract new members and eventually led to a split in the fellowship.

It is also likely that the Oxford Group's split, as well as other early examples of conflict in AA, helped to inspire Bill in his writing of the Ninth Tradition. AA needed service functions to support its work. How could it ensure that these services would be supplied without creating special committees and boards to be responsible for such services? Bill had already set up the General Service Office (GSO) in New York City, and the Alcoholic Foundation (which later became the General Service Board of Alcoholics Anonymous). But there was no direct connection to the AA membership. There had already been a flare-up when a founding member in Cleveland complained about book royalties being paid to Bill W. and Dr. Bob. Though this was settled amicably, it was an example of the kind of rebellion that could occur. Such conflicts could tear AA apart and perhaps undermine its mission.

Bill was always very concerned about AA's future; so much so that when he first introduced the Traditions in the April 1946 *A.A. Grapevine* he called them "Twelve Points to Assure Our Future."[5] Perhaps if AA members today meditated on the significance of that statement, "to assure our future," when listening to the Traditions being read at a meeting, they would understand the importance Bill placed on these "Points" and might more readily accept the responsibility that the pioneers entrusted to the fellowship.

Both Bill and Dr. Bob saw the need for a General Service Conference, and they recognized that the AA Trustees should be voted in by a group of delegates representing the groups. One of the concerns that led directly to the formation of the conference was the understanding that future decisions for AA unity must come from the members. This twist was certainly different from any typical business structure or government.

The unity and future of AA was to be placed on each member equally, virtually guaranteeing that a member selected to "serve" truly would serve and not govern.

This conference would cover all of North America, and simply be a larger form of "the committees and boards responsible to those they serve." With the assistance of Bernard Smith, a nonalcoholic trustee who was also an attorney, Bill laid down a plan for such a conference. This required careful thought and understanding, though, because some AA members were suspicious of a new concept being added to a fellowship that already worked well. Some objections were reportedly being voiced in Akron, where AA launched in 1935. What did Dr. Bob have to say about a General Service Conference? With only a few months to live, did he feel that Bill was taking the fellowship beyond the "Keep it simple" stage?

Actually, it was Dr. Bob's fatal illness that prompted Bill to move faster in offering this concept to the fellowship. With some contributions from Dr. Bob, Bill developed a pamphlet, which was introduced to the fellowship just one month before Bob's death. It was entitled *The General Service Conference of Alcoholics Anonymous — Your Third Legacy, Will You Accept It?* by Dr. Bob and Bill, dated October 1950.

In June of 1955, the AA delegates met at the Springfield Hotel in St. Louis just before the twentieth anniversary celebration at the International Convention, held the beginning of July. It was there that Bill formally presented *The Third Legacy Manual* to the delegates. It was later renamed *The Service Manual*.

It was five years after Bob's death that Bill toured cities in North America to present the idea to large groups. Dr. Bob's death in November of 1950 was a sad warning to AA members that the founders would not be around to guide the fellowship forever.

As Bill presented it, "The Third Legacy" was the service responsibility being bequeathed to the general membership. From its founders, AA had received the two legacies of recovery and unity. Now service was added, which the AA membership would facilitate through the General Service Conference. Bill's gift was to establish such a conference without transforming it into an oppressive governing body. Indeed, the theme of the first meeting of the General Service Conference was "not to govern, but to serve." This theme was chosen by Bill, and it underscored his determination to avoid the creation of a dictatorial controlling body.

The first panel of delegates met in New York in April of 1951, and Bill was pleased to note that at least one-third of them were old-timers in the program. The rest had between four and eight years' sobriety. Most of them had also been chosen by a two-thirds vote, a stipulation Bill had proposed to avoid the bitter politics of close elections.

By 1955, when AA had its Second International Convention in St. Louis, Bill formally stepped down from the fellowship's service responsibility. This in effect ceded it to the now well-established General Service Conference. AA, through its delegates, now had the responsibility for the General Service Board of AA, the General Service Office in New York, and AA's publishing operations, including the *A.A. Grapevine*. One wag said of Bill's leaving that "Bill would spend the next fifteen years stepping down."[6]

There was some truth in this witty comment, as AA leaders continued to look to Bill when issues came up. But when he died on January 24, 1971, part of his legacy was a fellowship that could survive and grow without his presence and leadership. If AA members wanted to know how Bill would respond to certain issues, it could usually be found in his writings.

As mentioned in an earlier chapter, members coming into AA today are immediately encouraged to get involved in service. In addition to making coffee and greeting newcomers, when the new member has been sober for a short while he or she may be asked to serve the group in some other capacity, as chairperson, general service representative, or any other available position.

These group services need organization and communication to make sure the group is able to function with some basic order, harmony, and unity. Most groups choose a rotation for all service positions, allowing members to have the opportunity to serve for a limited period of time. This helps to keep members "right-sized," keeping in mind that nobody is "Mr. or Ms. AA" and there are no bosses.

Many longtime members say it's unlikely they would have stayed sober if they hadn't had a service commitment in the beginning, something where others were counting on them, even if it was just to make the coffee. Perhaps this type of "giving of oneself to the service of others without expectation" is what Dr. Bob was referring to in his last public appearance at Cleveland in 1950. He said:

> **Our Twelve Steps, when simmered down to the last, resolve themselves into the words *love* and *service*.**[7]

Another interesting observation regarding service in AA is that nobody can really name which service is most important; some may think a delegate is, while others feel it must be a trustee. Within a group some might think it's the secretary who is most vital, when others feel it's the general service representative. The truth is that all these service positions are important in keeping AA together. Scores of sober members agree that the most important service role any alcoholic can perform is to extend to the next new member that same hand of kindness and consideration that was freely extended to them.

10
Staying Out
of the Fray

Throughout each chapter, there have been discussions of the Traditions as they were introduced at the First International Convention held in Cleveland in 1950. It is obvious that even then, the members had limited experience with the actual application of the Traditions. This was, in part, because they had just been introduced a few years earlier in the long form. This form was introduced in Cleveland and has been used ever since. George from Carlsbad, discussing Tradition Ten seemed a little confused about this topic, but his excellent points are worth considering today.

16 On Tradition Ten: "Alcoholics Anonymous has no opinion on outside issues; hence the A.A. name ought never be drawn into public controversy." That is a very important Tradition, and one that could be abused. In my own case, and I say that because I am a human being with all the frailties of mankind even though I have spent

several years trying to follow the AA program, there are
many times that I have been called on as a speaker. I
have been in [the] public light at times, not as a speaker,
but as a singer. And I still have that "actor's ego."

And I thought it might be a good time here to use
my name, and get a little billing here... I see now the
wisdom and the good old common sense in all of our
Traditions. Today, the names of our speakers on the
platform are mentioned to you. You ought to know who
we are, and where we came from. It's right, and good
for the work. But when we reach public level, then
rightfully, we must keep our anonymity. In my humble
opinion, anonymity is the great spiritual gift that AA
has possessed all throughout its life, and the spiritual
marvel that will lead us down through Tradition forever.
Thank you.[1]

Bill W. and Dr. Bob both had strong political opinions, as well as views on religion. In his drinking days,
Bill wrote letters on political issues, while Dr. Bob
expressed himself on government involvement in the
medical field. However, neither of their opinions on
either politics or religion ever found their way into
AA. From the society's very beginning, it became clear
that recovered alcoholics had to keep public controversies out of the fellowship. This has clearly protected
AA's unity, while avoiding the bitter fights that fester
throughout the world.

This was not an easy thing for Bill, and there must
have been times when he was tempted to use his stature

in AA to promote or oppose certain causes. He also had to resist the urge to strike back when a few members attacked what they perceived as his political views. He and his devoted secretary, Nell Wing, sometimes had heated arguments about current political issues.[2] He would later apologize when, at times, he would become too angry in stating views that conflicted with hers. None of that went beyond the office.

How did Bill feel about certain political issues? Some of the early AA members thought that his views "went back to McKinley." Since this was never explained, we can only infer that Bill generally favored freedom for business, and was suspicious of government interventions. While still drinking, he even wrote letters opposing government involvement in public utilities. He also had no interest in seeking government help or subsidies of any kind for alcoholics.

We can also believe that Bill and the other pioneers were still feeling the open wounds that Prohibition had dealt to the country. Many of them had done their drinking illegally, obtaining their supplies from friendly bootleggers or illegal taverns called *speakeasies*. Bill never expressed an opinion about Prohibition, except to see it as an "ill-starred" controversy. The Big Book does cast doubt on any scheme attempting to help the alcoholic by interfering with his supply.

Nothing in Tradition Ten has any bearing on an individual's right to engage in various controversies. It does suggest that the AA name should not be drawn into outside issues. If individual members are involved in these issues, it should be done in such a way that does not include AA.

That might even include times when AA as a whole comes under attack. Such a test came in 1963, when the previously mentioned national magazine cover story was published calling AA a cult and declaring that it had veered from its goal of helping alcoholics. Written by a man whose credentials included a doctorate from Columbia University, the article angered hundreds of AA members around the country. Some of them sent the magazine bitter letters of protest. There were also demands that Bill W. and AA's General Service Office in New York should fire back a rebuttal.

Bill W. took a different approach, however, that reflected the principles of Tradition Ten. Though the magazine article was about AA, the topic presented had little to do with the everyday activities of AA members and groups. He authored an article for the *A.A. Grapevine* entitled, "Our Critics Can Be Our Benefactors." This article addressed the topic without directly naming either the magazine or the author. Read today, decades after the critical article was published, Bill's reply addressed the principles underlying the Tenth Tradition while avoiding any argument with points that the offending author had raised.

It turned out that Bill had already anticipated the likely appearance of such an article. He even quoted what he had previously written in "Twelve Concepts for World Service."

Let us suppose that A.A. does fall under sharp public attack or heavy ridicule; and let us take the particular case where such pronouncements happen to have little or no justification in fact.

Almost without exception it can be confidently esti-mated that our best defense in these situations would be no defense whatever — namely, complete silence at the public level. Unreasonable people are stimulated all the more by opposition. If in good humor we leave them strictly alone, they are apt to subside the more quickly.[3]

As it turned out, the public and AA furor over the article quickly subsided. There appeared to be no damage to the fellowship or its ability to carry out its primary purpose. Although the critic had suggested that AA was no longer effective, its membership today is up tenfold from the 200,000 members AA had in 1963.[4] In the meantime, other critics of AA have voiced their beliefs; there are even some websites devoted to criticism of the fellowship. Neither the General Service Conference nor the General Service Office responds to these criticisms. In the meantime, there have been countless controversies about the use of alcohol and other drugs covered in the media, with public argu-ments raging about everything from the legalization of marijuana to the effectiveness of the war on drugs, to what should be the legal limit of blood alcohol content to drive. No AA members are known to have joined in such controversies, at least in ways that would involve AA. It has probably become general knowledge that AA expresses no opinion on these kinds of issues, and so its members and World Service are not likely to be contacted for comments. AA provides general information about the fellowship and its history and leaves other issues alone.

The fate of the Washingtonians, and how their involvement in controversial issues quickly led to their demise, provides a good object lesson for people in AA who might question the need for this Tradition. Not only should the AA name not be drawn into public controversy, the other Traditions show that the AA name should not be drawn out in public in any manner that endorses or promotes other entities or issues. This applies at the individual member level as well in that members are asked to protect their anonymity at the public level in Traditions Eleven and Twelve.

In Bill W.'s closing talk at the 1950 Cleveland Convention, he shared the following comments. Although they are not entirely related to this particular Tradition, they are relevant to the basic principle of AA unity (Tradition One), with focus on its primary purpose (Tradition Five) and anonymity (Traditions Eleven and Twelve) that the Tenth Tradition supports.

> There's another Tradition we have, which does not go without controversy. In Alcoholics Anonymous, you'll find lots of controversy. Sometimes we act like hell. We can be very cruel sometimes. We can be very thoughtless. Sometimes we gossip maliciously. Sometimes we quarrel violently over our small business affairs. This is no perfect

society; we have many standards. But from the very beginning, by some deep and sure instinct, this society has known that it could never quarrel over the issues of politics, sectarian religion, alcohol reform, and the like. I have never heard in AA a bitter religious or political argument.

We shall have to be ever more on the guard against these things. But to these real threats, I'm confident we shall never succumb; we've got our matter of relating ourselves to the world outside. Oh, alcoholics are the greatest promoters in the world. And yet isn't it a remarkable fact that out of all of us salesmen, you can't find five people in the whole society of Alcoholics Anonymous who get their names and pictures printed in the newspapers nowadays?

We realize that we must place principles before personalities. We see anonymity as a token of our group humility; as the greatest protection that we have. I must confess that I myself once upon a time disagreed with every single one of these Traditions to some extent or other. I have violated them, nearly all, at times. At other times I have been tempted to violate them, and then the group conscience has spoken out to me, and said, "No, Bill, you can't do this thing to us. What you propose is good, perhaps, but it is not good enough. Aren't you the fellow who has forever said, 'Sometimes the good is the enemy of the best'?" [5]

There are both AA members and non-AA members who feel that this Tradition and several others are from the "horse and buggy days," that AA should keep up with the tempo of the times. Why, with two million members

AA could exercise considerable clout in the political and religious arenas. What harm could it do if the AA organization expressed an opinion on outside issues? Some think AA could do a great deal of good if it were to collectively sound a unified voice.

Certainly AA members have strong opinions on every issue; just ask almost any member who will win a sporting event or a political election, or ask for his or her view on an environmental issue. Although the Tradition states that "Alcoholics Anonymous has no opinion on outside issues," it by no means creates some sort of expectation that members shouldn't have an opinion. The key here is that members don't speak for AA. It is also generally recognized as a good practice to not discuss controversial or outside issues in the AA meeting. This could easily cause friction and divert the group away from its primary purpose.

On occasion a speaker will drift from the topic and begin voicing his or her personal agenda. When this happens, the group most often practices love and tolerance. If the behavior continues, usually the chairperson guides the speaker back to the topic. In some cases group members talk with the individual and suggest that the AA philosophy of "no opinion on outside issues" is respected.

One issue you're likely to hear AA members express strong opinions about is that of reading or using nonconference-approved literature. Some members are of the opinion that AA approves and disapproves literature, which isn't true. Since AA began, members are encouraged to read anything they want; if it helps them stay sober, all the better. AA simply has no opinion.

So, why is there conference-approved literature? AA began publishing literature in 1939 under the name Works Publishing Company, which became AA Publishing in the early 1950s, and now uses the name of the governing organization, Alcoholics Anonymous World Services. Until the early 1990s, all literature published by AA displayed the circle and triangle logo. This was phased out and replaced with the words Conference Approved. This statement is now found on literature published by AA.

Many groups prefer to stick to conference-approved literature to preserve consistency of message about the Steps, Traditions, and AA history. Still, each group is autonomous, and the group conscience eventually decides what literature the groups sell and read at their meetings.

Another outside issue occasionally brought into AA is the use of medications such as anti-depressants. Some years ago, many members believed that no one should take any psychiatric medications because they are mood-altering. However, AA never had a policy regarding medication and in fact has published conference-approved literature affirming the legitimacy of psychiatric medications for the treatment of emotional illness. Yet, there are still some members who claim that if you take these types of medications, you're not sober, even though it is well established that AA makes no such claim and no member is qualified to speak for AA. Most people in AA now accept that these are individual matters to be handled by each member and his or her doctor.

Many of these outside issues that find their way into meetings can generate strong opinions and feelings; they are complex and are not easy to deal with since there is no cookie-cutter process that works for every situation. Hopefully, good sponsorship and consulting the Big Book and Twelve and Twelve will help the members make decisions that are in the best interest of everyone. Many sober members have found, through the Steps, the answers they seek. When Bill wrote his essay on Step Eleven he shared as follows:

> *There is a direct linkage among self-examination, meditation, and prayer. Taken separately, these practices can bring much relief and benefit. But when they are logically related and interwoven, the result is an unshakable foundation for life. Now and then we may be granted a glimpse of that ultimate reality which is God's kingdom. And we will be comforted and assured that our own destiny in that realm will be secure for so long as we try, however falteringly, to find and do the will of our own Creator.*[6]

Conforming to AA's Traditions requires self-sacrifice at some level, even if that means letting go and allowing others to make decisions one might disagree with. Too often old character defects resist this type of ego reduction and the personal sacrifice necessary to accommodate these principles. Clearly, AAs can benefit from practicing the slogan "Live and let live."

11
Anonymity: A Key to AA's Survival

*L*ate in the year 1970, three months before his passing, AA cofounder Bill W. issued what became his last message to the fellowship. This message actually went on to become a strong reminder of the importance of abiding by the anonymity principle addressed in the Eleventh Tradition.

Bill's farewell message was read by Lois at the annual celebration of his birthday in New York, this having been his thirty-sixth year of sobriety. Lois then framed this message, and it is displayed on the wall at Stepping Stones, the historic home of Bill and Lois Wilson. The message read:

> *My dear friends,*
>
> *Recently an AA member sent me an unusual greeting, which I would like to extend to you. He told me it was an ancient Arabian salutation. Perhaps we have no Arabian groups, but it still seems a fitting expression of how I feel*

for each of you. It says, "I salute you and thank you for your life."

My thoughts are much occupied these days with gratitude to our Fellowship and for the myriad blessings bestowed upon us by God's Grace.

If I were asked which of these blessings I felt was most responsible for our growth as a Fellowship and most vital to our continuity, I would say, the "Concept of Anonymity." Anonymity has two attributes that are essential to our individual and collective survival; the spiritual, and the practical.

On the spiritual level, anonymity demands the greatest discipline of which we are capable; on the practical level, anonymity has brought protection for the newcomer, respect and support of the world outside, and security from those of us who would use AA for sick and selfish purposes.

AA must and will continue to change with the passing years. We cannot turn back the clock, nor should we. However, I deeply believe that the principle of anonymity must remain our primary and enduring safeguard. As long as we accept our sobriety in our traditional spirit of anonymity, we will continue to receive God's Grace.

And so — once more, I salute you in that spirit, and again I thank you for your lives. May God bless us all, now and forever.[1]

Bill emphasized the extreme importance of AA's Eleventh and Twelfth Traditions, which really gave the society its name. Tradition Eleven was referred to as the practical one, while Tradition Twelve is considered the spiritual one. It would be difficult to find principles more vital to AA's existence than these. Yet they are sometimes disregarded by individuals who do not seem to understand the true meaning of anonymous: not disclosing one's own AA membership or another's at the public level.

Tradition Eleven makes this very clear:

> *Our public relations policy is based on attraction rather than promotion; we need always maintain personal anonymity at the level of press, radio, and films.*[2]

AA's other cofounder, Dr. Bob, passed away in October 1950. By this time, membership had risen to more than 100,000, and AA had begun to receive an abundance of favorable press from cities across the United States as well as many overseas. The success of the AA movement was real, and this new society of former drunks seemed to have the answer for alcoholism. Movie companies wanted to get in on the action, as did radio and television shows. During this period newspapers and national magazines ran pieces on AA in every city. AA membership numbers continued to grow, and by 1953 Bill W. claimed that more than half the membership had come from the publicity from these sources.

There were several factors that seemed to draw this publicity: the alcoholics were anonymous (at least for the most part), and AA wasn't seeking the attention. The press usually respected AA's wishes to remain anonymous but were nevertheless thrilled to tell the AA story. In 1956, Bill W. was interviewed on the New York talk show *Weekday*. The host was Mike Wallace, who later went on to fame as one of the hosts on the news program 60 *Minutes*. The interview began with Wallace's co-host saying, "Today we've agreed to 'no last names.'"

The picture of AA looks much different today due to the explosive growth of the fellowship. Since Bill W.'s death in 1971, the name Alcoholics Anonymous has entered into the public conscience in practically every corner of the world. In some cities and within certain groups of people, it has almost become a mark of distinction or prestige to be in recovery as a member of AA or NA. This is unlike the early days, when fifty percent of the members coming into AA were through word of mouth and media publicity. Beginning in the early 1970s, members arrived from many different sources, including treatment facilities and the court system.

Since such a large number of new members still are coming into AA through these third-party facilities and agencies, some members fear AA is losing its effectiveness. One effect in recent years has been a major decline in AA Twelve Step calls where an alcoholic or a family member might call the local AA wanting help. Two members would then go directly out to call on the alcoholic and tell their stories of recovery to encourage the person to join AA. Today when these people are desperate, they are more likely to call professional interventionists, treatment facilities, and addiction or mental health professionals before they call AA.

Still, the success of AA has been so astonishing that most medical professionals, counselors, treatment facilities, courts, and even prison systems immediately introduce their clients to AA. Many treatment facilities even make attendance of an AA meeting part of their program. Of course, AA has no official opinion on any of these agencies, and the AA Traditions clearly state that the policy be of cooperation and not affiliation.

Several questions arise in the examination of this process in regard to the Eleventh Tradition: Is this attraction or promotion? Do these matters fall under AA's public relations policy, or is public relations exclusive to the media? A quick look at the social networking component that has surfaced in recent years is enough to make any Tradition-minded member uneasy.

How do these new challenges really affect AA? Do they at all? One member recently shared a story. Someone had contacted him through his Facebook account with a message, asking, "Are you in AA?" He answered in the affirmative. The individual inquired about an AA meeting, started attending, and then found two years of continuing sobriety. The interesting thing about this particular story is that these two individuals have never met, and live more than a thousand miles apart.[3] There are many positive stories of how this new social media is creating opportunities for introductions into AA and other Twelve Step programs.

Some of this work may just be the new form of Twelve Step calls. Certainly the Tradition suggests that AA members should not promote themselves in public as members of Alcoholics Anonymous. With this in mind regarding social media, the Eleventh Tradition suggests that members should not identify themselves as an AA member. But they can make public statements that they were in a treatment program, are in recovery, or have participated in a Twelve Step program, provided that they don't publically break their anonymity specific to their membership in AA.

The social-networking sites have private groups, and there are established online meetings where members disclose amongst each other that they are in AA or another Twelve Step program. Because these groups are private and joined by invitation only, nongroup members can't see the conversations. These groups of members are not breaking anonymity at the public level. There will be a lot of discussion about the challenges to be faced with these new technologies and opportunities in the coming years.

Since there are Twelve Traditions, it is curious that Bill W. attached so much importance to the last two on the list. It could be observed that anonymity was being accepted as a guiding principle for AA, even before the Twelve Traditions were formally adopted by a vote at the First International Convention. This appears to have developed after the publication of the text *Alcoholics Anonymous* in 1939.

How well have AA members observed practical anonymity over the years? The records seem to show many well-publicized anonymity breaks since the late 1940s after AA had become recognized as an important institution in society. The members who broke their anonymity sometimes offered excuses, including the belief that by being publicized as recovered alcoholics, they were drawing people to the AA program.

One well-known case from the 1950s involved an actress, whose recovery story became a best-selling book, as well as a popular movie — a phenomenon that has become commonplace today. While some AA members objected to this anonymity break, others claimed that by her coming out as a recovered alcoholic publically, she certainly helped other women accept the program.

AA itself has neither the power nor the right to force members to observe personal anonymity, or even to respect the anonymity of others. The best thing society can do is to explain AA's anonymity Tradition to people in the media and other inquirers in the hope that they will respect it. It is also a common practice at large AA gatherings to ask the media to respect speakers' anonymity.

Some may argue that the world has changed so much that it is no longer necessary to preserve anonymity. Much of the stigma of being an alcoholic has faded away, partly because celebrities and other prominent people have openly admitted to being recovered alcoholics but also because addiction is being accepted as a "no fault" disease by more and more people. Some believe it is no longer necessary to maintain anonymity at any level; they want to shout their AA affiliation from the rooftops. Others urge caution in this regard, pointing out that public recoveries can also turn into public relapses that can hurt the reputation of not only the individual but also his or her treatment program or AA. AA members and addiction professionals accept relapse as a common phenomenon with this chronic condition, but to the uninformed general public, this can still be seen as a sign of failure.

A person's AA membership is usually his or her own business, and there is no justifiable reason that others should know about it. While some might applaud a person for finding recovery, there are still people who believe that addiction is in some way a permanent handicap. This might be particularly true in executive management. A person might be passed over for promotion simply because of a past history of excessive drinking. Even if one agrees to publicly disclose his or her own AA membership, it is always wrong to identify another as an AA member, even if that person agrees.

For a growing number of authors, musicians, movie stars, and others who in recent years have decided to disregard AA's Eleventh Tradition, it is time for AA to evolve and not live in the past, when addiction carried so much stigma. Anonymity is no longer essential in their eyes; they believe the benefits of allowing people to know you are a member of AA far outweigh the potential risks involved with public knowledge of one's membership in the fellowship.

In May of 2011, the *New York Times* published an article entitled "Challenging the Second 'A' in AA." In the article, the author openly expressed his membership in Alcoholics Anonymous, and listed the names of many others that he feels share the same views on anonymity. The article discusses various celebrities who have broken their anonymity and feel justified doing so. One statement he made about the Eleventh Tradition was, "More and more, anonymity seems like an anachronistic vestige of the Great Depression, when AA got its start and when alcoholism was seen as not just a weakness but a disgrace."[4]

The author also quotes AA members who have publicly broken their anonymity, claiming that it is "healthy that anonymity is fading."[5] While there may be some valid points addressed by this article and others like it, a closer look into the Traditions and especially the core principle of anonymity may reveal something more vital to quality recovery than these critics realize. Core to alcoholics working a successful Twelve Step program is their need to sacrifice their overinflated egos and practice the spiritual principle of humility. This development of humility allows alcoholics to remember their powerlessness over their addictions and the importance of surrender to a Higher Power in working a spiritual program. The Eleventh Tradition positions anonymity as a foundation to a spiritual program in discouraging self-promotion and encouraging "walking the walk" more than "talking the talk." And the Twelfth Tradition, discussed in the next chapter, leads the members to the understanding and application of placing principles before personalities.

Continuing in the format of previous chapters, following is more of the transcription of the talk given at the First International Convention held in Cleveland in 1950. This summation was presented by Kylie, a member from Boston who was selected to discuss Tradition Eleven.

17 Through most of the previous discussion about Traditions, these two have been talked about [most]. Because I think they're the background of all we have to offer. The most important thing about AA is what we have to offer. We have to offer security to a beaten, broken-down, defeated, frustrated alcoholic — that's all; a home, shelter. In all these matters I can only interpret them with relationship to Kylie [himself]. Why? I don't know. It isn't that he's very important, but I can't seem to interpret them as how they would affect you. But I can insofar as they affect me.

To show you what I mean, in my latest revision of the Twelve Steps, as from time to time I will revise them — so far no one has published any of my revisions, by the way — I have taken out the personal pronouns "we" and "our" and substituted "I" and "my." This is for a very, very, very good reason. Over the years, I've become an expert diagnostician of other people's failings, and that doesn't do very much good. I have become very adept at confessing other people's sins and weaknesses, and that doesn't do very much good for Kylie. So I think the Step should say "I made a decision to turn my will over to the care of God as I understand him," because I can't speak for "we."

Why do I bring this out? I bring this out because my drinking, which I think perhaps had something to do with my alcoholism, came as a result of certain people not being willing to make adjustments on themselves. I would have been all right, but they wouldn't conform. "They" included many people, my wife, my employer. At times I took on some very worthwhile adversaries, like the Roman Catholic Church. They had a few weaknesses, which they wouldn't change, and that resulted in alcoholism for Kylie. The United States Navy was a fairly tough outfit too, so I tackled them for a while. I gave them a hell of a run for it too. Even in AA I found that certain people needed to adjust themselves.

As time went on, I learned that any progress that would be made would be made as a result of Kylie making adjustments on Kylie; God, what a bitter lesson. It was brutal. It was almost worse than drinking, and believe me, that was bad. But that was the only way there would be any progress.

So with regard to these Traditions, how are we going to enforce them? Are we going to set up spy committees to see who goes out and makes a little cut someplace in the name of AA? Sometimes we forget that we have a membership of 100,000. That's a good stand for fraud, con men, phonies — I don't know what you might call them. This is after they are through drinking. I'm not talking about when they are drinking; then they're pretty good people. This is after they get through. How shall we rule them, how shall we rule you? Get that? We shall rule you if Kylie makes adjustments on Kylie.

A few years ago down at the Yale School for Alcoholic Studies, Bill was submitted to a question-and-answer period after giving a talk about AA government. A Baptist minister got up and said words something like this... (It seems as though he had some deacons and a board of directors to contend with, and that they weren't making the proper adjustments) and he said, "This is all a wonderful government and organization; having just enough organization to prevent organization is a wonderful thing. I'd really like to take it and transplant it into my church."

Basically he was saying, "So that these babies will mind their own business and let me run this thing the way it should be run." He didn't say that, but clearly that's what he meant. "Tell me how I can do that?" I thought that was a tough question, and I thought he'd have Bill pretty well wrapped up. I didn't know what he was going to say. I thought he was going to give them the old "razza-matazz," you know, that "Easy does it" routine when he doesn't have the answer....

But Bill thought for a moment, and he slowly said to the guy, "I think I've got the answer for ya." He said, "You find some way to get the bite on your parishioners, like John Barleycorn has got the bite on us, and you won't need any laws or rules and regulations."

I've come to find out, if I don't [make adjustments on Kylie], John Barleycorn, in all probability, will again put the bite on me, and I'll be back where I started; and it's too long of a road back, believe me.

So with these Traditions, I'm sure that is how we'll enforce them. I will help to promote AA publicity by attraction, not by promotion. By living the kind of life where people say, "Well...something has happened;

lightning struck and the bum is sober, but for God's sakes keep quiet and don't mess with it. He belongs to something. I don't know what it is, let him stay the hell in there, don't get him out." That is publicity by attraction, believe me.

I don't want to bore you with too many details about myself, but God has been good. I have been a very, very lucky guy. Things have happened to me that I can explain in no other way; there is no other explanation for them except for that's the way it should be.

It's a privilege for me that I have been forced into a position where I am the chairman of a board of a public body that is going to spend two hundred million dollars in the next four years. Can you imagine tossing the Kylie of old into a job like that? Can you imagine the terrific responsibility that the whole community in which I live has, knowing that I am an ex-drunk? It's a matter of public record. Everybody knows it. I can't walk down the street and say, "I'm in church now, and I used to be a drunk." They know.

I don't mean by that that I publicly allow my name to be used and say, "The great Kylie is now a member of Alcoholics Anonymous." No, that isn't the way it's done. But people know, people have a way of finding out; particularly when you're tossed into a position like that. And I say literally tossed for no good reason that I can think of. Nothing to do with ability, nothing to do with talent; but just that's the way it should be. It puts a...burden on my shoulders. Because, you know, as human beings being what they are, in and out of AA, people like to see the heads of the great fall. It might be quite an event in some people's lives if Kylie did go back to drinking....

The great lesson for me down through the years in AA I have had a crowd of guys around me, my friends — at times, I didn't know that was the word for them, but now I know that it is — who have been great deflators, who have been able to keep me in line, who have been really very, very good for me. They are still my friends. That's why it's very simple for me to have the most important thing in my whole life being to submerge myself as just another drunk in this great organization.[6]

After the Traditions were introduced in Cleveland by the six members, Bill W. shared a summary on all the Traditions. Bill's comments on Tradition Eleven effectively summarize the points addressed in this chapter. This was how Bill closed out the session on the Traditions:

18 "Our public relations policy is based on attraction rather than promotion; we need always maintain personal anonymity at the level of press, radio and films." Or the last one again, emphasizing the spiritual variety of anonymity. "Anonymity is the spiritual foundation of all our Traditions, ever reminding us to place principles above personalities."

Let me tell you one more story of a great temptation I had. The book was under preparation, and we had no title for it. Somebody suggested the name *Alcoholics Anonymous*. For months we had meetings and voted on titles. Nobody cared too much for that title. At long last, the day approached that we had to name the book; that title got to be very, very popular. At first I liked the idea. And then something, which certainly was not of God, began speaking to me and saying, "Bill, why shouldn't you sign that book? After all, authors sign books; you've written the text. Sure, the other fellows wrote stories, but you know the text is the important thing. Why don't you sign that book?"

At that time the most popular title in the voting was a title called, "The Way Out." And I thought to myself, "Well, why not 'The Way Out,' by Bill Wilson?"...Then I had even another thought, forgetting dear old Smithy, the rock on whom this movement is founded, I said to myself, "Why shouldn't this be called The Wilson Movement?" When I came in to our little meeting, where we were talking about these titles, and tactfully insinuated these ideas of signing the book and The Wilson Movement, I got that very stony stare, and the group conscience again spoke and it said, "No, you can't do this thing to us. Aren't you the guy who has so often said, 'The good is the enemy of the best'?" So it became *Alcoholics Anonymous*.

Years later, the March of Dimes did a newsreel about us; I was in the projection room. An official of the company said, "Bill, do you realize that this film is going to be shown to twelve million people? That twelve million people who knew little or nothing about Alcoholics Anonymous are now going to find out?" Then that film aired, and as it rolled, the book *Alcoholics Anonymous* was held up to view two or three times. I looked at it, and I must confess that I cried like a baby; thinking how much wiser my fellows had been than me; asking myself, "Had this been called 'The Way Out,' by Bill Wilson, would the March of Dimes show this society to twelve million people? Of course not; thank God it's *Alcoholics Anonymous*. Thank God for the conscience of this movement, which corrected me. Thank God it's *Alcoholics Anonymous*. Period.[7]

12

**Principles
Before
Personalities**

Tradition Twelve's anonymity is the spiritual foundation of all of our Traditions, ever reminding us to place "principles before personalities." When Bill W. authored the book *Twelve Steps and Twelve Traditions,* he had the experience of not only having lived sober for a little more than fifteen years, he had also seen the AA principles working in his life and the lives of hundreds of others.

If you were to study Bill's life, you would quickly see how concerned he was for the sober alcoholic who continued to suffer. Perhaps this was because of his personal battles with depression. Bill witnessed firsthand alcoholics who had practiced the AA program, but still seemed to be unhappy. He addressed some of these issues with the AA doctors through his correspondences regarding the use of vitamin B_3 (also known as niacin). Bill and several of his AA friends became interested in using massive doses of the vitamin; they found great relief and an enhanced sense of well-being.

The niacin therapy was done during the last ten years of Bill's life; both he and Lois took high levels of the vitamin daily. Of course this had nothing to do with AA, and Bill respected the Traditions and the wishes of his friends on the General Service Board by keeping this research out of AA.

In a video interview available on Youtube.com, the late Dr. Abram Hoffer, M.D. (a Canadian biochemist and psychiatrist who worked with Bill on the niacin research project) discussed the project and indicated that Bill was certainly onto something using niacin to treat depression. Dr. Hoffer, along with his partner Dr. Humphrey Osmond, had been researching the use of niacin for the treatment of schizophrenics.

Hoffer also said when speaking of Bill W., "I learned more from him about addiction than from any other single source." He credited Bill with having helped him to start the first SA (Schizophrenics Anonymous) in Saskatoon, Saskatchewan. [1]

Looking back, it is easy to see many examples of Bill's humility and personal sacrifice. We've already talked about the early example of his declining the opportunity to become a paid lay therapist at Towns Hospital, where he had his spiritual experience. Throughout his life he gave credit to others while deferring it for himself. He would often say, "AA has many founders." This may have been true in some sense, but it was a statement made with humility. Bill was the principal author of the basic text *Alcoholics Anonymous, Twelve Steps and Twelve Traditions*, the service structure, the concepts, and hundreds of articles. There were other contributors to the AA movement and its early success, but Bill was undoubtedly the engine that pulled the train.

Of course he was human, and alcoholic, and would often point out his own character defects. Some folks have considered him a saint, but Bill would not have agreed with those people. After his death he was recognized by *Time* magazine as one of the top one hundred people of the century. In all likelihood, he would have declined that honor, as he did so many others. Bill was quick to give God the credit for the good works he had done through the AA movement. His favorite prayer was that of St. Francis.

Prayer of Saint Francis of Assisi

Lord, make me an instrument of your peace.
Where there is hatred, let me sow love;
where there is injury, pardon;
where there is doubt, faith;
where there is despair, hope;
where there is darkness, light;
and where there is sadness, joy.

O Divine Master, grant that I may not so much seek
to be consoled as to console;
to be understood as to understand;
to be loved as to love.
For it is in giving that we receive;
it is in pardoning that we are pardoned;
and it is in dying that we are born to eternal life. Amen.

In his writing on the Twelfth Tradition he said,

> *The spiritual substance of anonymity is sacrifice. Because A.A.'s Twelve Traditions repeatedly ask us to give up personal desires for the common good, we realize that the sacrificial spirit — well symbolized by anonymity — is the foundation of them all. It is A.A.'s proved willingness to make sacrifices that gives people their high confidence in our future.* [2]

Seven years after the publication of *Twelve Steps and Twelve Traditions*, Bill expanded on his views regarding the Traditions in his talk at the Long Beach International Convention, in 1960. He spent considerable time on the Twelfth Tradition, sharing some of his most intimate thoughts regarding humility through the principle of anonymity. Because most of this information has never been published, we have decided to share the transcription of his entire talk on the Twelfth Tradition and anonymity as he related it to the spiritual foundation of AA.

> What a lucky break that word, *anonymity*, the deep spiritual bearing of it. That last Tradition is most intimately and spiritually related to the first, which intrigues us no matter what our concern and tenderness for the individual may be. The common welfare is first. Underlying all of these Traditions in their several aspects and functions is a deep spiritual significance of anonymity. I don't mean technical anonymity; no names and pictures in the

newspapers please, those are just the mechanics of what we are talking about here; in the protection of our very fallible people is neither shame nor false modesty. It is recognition that in us the old forces may revive. The greatest protection against them is the sacrifice of even legitimate aspirations.

God expects us to try to be reasonably secure. He hopes that we shall be somebody in the right way. The leadership of the world is or should be dependent upon people who have had those aspirations, and who work publicly for freedom under God; thereby qualifying themselves in leadership of us all. For us, we know there are special dangers; these are the forces that brought us to the pit. Therefore our security, our general welfare, and indeed our spiritual estate and its ultimate value are going to depend upon the willingness of each and every one of us to sacrifice at the public level; these perfectly legitimate aspirations, which other people may have.

That is the token of the spirit, not of martyrdom; not of false humility, not of affected nobility. Let's just give up a little something to secure the destiny of Alcoholics Anonymous. The extent to which we have been able to do this with scarcely any deviation, under an immense and ever growing temptation as the AA name becomes a household word... I'm so grateful; here is our shield.

There is no more subtle form, perhaps no more destructive form of pride than the sort of pride that brags of its humility and its nobility of purpose. So what I am now about to do is something I have debated a lot about. It has to do with the contribution, which Dr. Bob and I, not for any excessive humility or nobility, began to do in the year in which he died. And he, in this all-important spiritual adventure, was the leader, and the bright example of greatness in spirit and action.

As you know the old boy had the CA [cancer], and after a while, his number certainly was up; Anne had gone. So I went often to Akron, and we used the phone a lot, and I hope I said last night that we never had an angry difference of opinion and we had a division of duties and responsibilities. There was a kinship there that I should probably never have with anybody. Bob was conservative and prudent, but never the fearful, I might add. I'm by nature kind of a gambler; risks are exciting. Bob was a spiritual natural; but the history of my life was an insensate pursuit of approval, prestige, and finally power.

Early in the history of this society I began to be told what I might not do by the group conscience. I will always remember the day when we were pretty poor; there on Clinton Street, some of the other boys getting on their feet and getting good jobs. I was up at Charlie Towns Hospital, and Charlie beckoned me into his office and he showed me the balance sheet, in the gold rush days of the 1920s, thousands of dollars a month.

Charlie said, "Look, Bill, your folks are getting on their feet, but you and Lois are starving to death. Why don't you move the operation in here? I'll give you a break on the profits. I'll give you a drawing account." Well, from his point of view, and from any outside point of view, this was a generous and legitimate proposition. As I went home, I felt kind of good. I could see Lois coming out of that department store. l could see a place to like, a place to go, some security.

Lois was cooking when l got home and the drunks were hungrily looking in the door; none of them paying any board. We were big hearted with no money. That was one way you could feed the ego in those days, you know. In those days, an AA could go to an AA dentist and say, "I'm an AA; l want my teeth filled." No cost, everything's free; same with the coal bill.

Well anyways, l broke the glad news. But Lois wasn't so quick on the uptake. Then the meeting started down in the parlor a little later. l told the boys of the glowing opportunity, and as l went on they got more restless. l could see that they didn't want to say anything, but finally one of them knew they had to. He said, "Bill, we know the state you folks are in here, but Bill, this thing rests on its good will. No professional could ever do this job of therapy. You can't do this to us." So l spoke to the group conscious, and l obeyed for the first time. As these Traditions developed, every one was contrary to my world of power, and I've had to learn obedience.

l might also say, before we come to the conclusion, that when these nonalcoholic friends of ours together formed the trusteeship, it was recognition that Bob and l couldn't do this job of world service. We had once, of course, begun to delegate them. Everything that AA possesses is of a service nature; its service money, its literature, its magazine — all came into their keeping legally. l have frequently been over there with some awful strong arguments, and l have been voted down. l don't even have a vote there, and this has been a hell of a good thing for me. This makes me interject right here, that this in the administrative sense of our greatest affairs is the working group conscious of Alcoholics Anonymous, and here they sit. In them and in their successors, I am sure we can have confidence and we can solve that critical problem of the transferring of the symbolist service leadership from Dr. Bob and myself. In your hands, and in theirs, our destiny can and will be secure, and that long since, AA has been safe, even for me.

But when Dr. Bob was dying, and this trusteeship did not have the stature that it now has, AA wasn't safe for me. One afternoon I went in to Dr. Bob's parlor, just to comfort him in his remaining hours, full of my altercations with the trustees. He brushed that off and he said, "Bill, you know a very touching thing has happened. An awful affecting thing and yet it has its comical aspect, just let me show you this." He got out a long roll of paper and unrolled it. It took up a big space on the floor, and in this was the architect's drawing of a dandy mausoleum in which he could be planted along with Annie as a founder.

Bob looked at it and his smile was broad, actually that guy could be good humored about even dying. Then he said, "I've been thinking quite a bit about this, Bill. Why for God's sake don't you and me get buried like other people?" This was not too serious, but the impact, the implications for me immediately became clear. This was the beginning of the enlargement of the Tradition of Alcoholics Anonymous. Not only to abjure from public recognition, but to refrain from public honors for AA work.

Soon after Dr. Bob had gone, I got word from my old alma mater from which I never graduated; and from which I would have been thrown out for poor scholarship had the World War not intervened. All of a sudden my dear, old alma mater thought I should have a degree for being one of the world's leading drunks. It wasn't a very big college, and it wasn't a very big degree.

I thought of Dr. Bob and, well, I said, "I guess not." Well then along came another one, and this one wasn't a very big college either, and that was pretty easy. Then came the great Lasker Award, and every fifth guy that had the Lasker Award got the Nobel Prize; this was the route to Stockholm. Well, it was offered to me. They always give it to individuals, and this time we had a near miss. But again, we remembered Dr. Bob, this "getting buried like other people."

So we got to angle it around so that it would be a Citation to Alcoholics Anonymous, recognition of us as a fellowship and not an honor to an individual. The San Francisco Opera House was filled, and our friends and drunks were standing in the aisles and hanging off the rafters. Down came the Governor and all these distinguished people, and Bernie Smith, then the nonalcoholic treasurer of the board received this Citation on behalf of AA. And I found myself in the talk of 120 seconds, something unheard of, in which I thanked them also. That was much better, wasn't it?

A couple of years later, a committee of rather distinguished-looking gentlemen awaited me in my office. With appropriate emphasis, dignity and enthusiasm, they said that they had come from their university, which was one of the oldest and greatest in this country. They said that on behalf of the corporation, the board of trustees so to speak, they wished to say that the university wished to confer upon me a Doctor of Laws degree.

Well, for a stockbroker and a drunk, this seemed like a really good going; when I looked up and found that a Doctor of Law degree was just about all that a big university could give to someone. The company of people in the world who had held these degrees as laymen was pretty small, and to say the least, distinguished. I felt the old emotions arise. At last spirituality had really paid off! And then I thought of Dr. Bob.

I thought, "Well, if the Lasker Award was the route to Stockholm, what in God's name could we do with this one?" And then I thought of Dr. Bob. So I began to ask people and a lot of people said to me, "Well, Bill, you deserve this, but that isn't the most important thing. The important thing is that this would give a standing to this society. That it would immediately give it a place in the world which would bring us support that we don't have; members perhaps beyond count. It's your duty to do this."

That sounded good. So we went over to the conscience of the movement in such matters, these fellows here, and we took a canvass of them. I guess they'll confess it has them a little rattled too. Some thought I should and some thought I shouldn't and some said, "Let's think about it."

On this board we have a very distinguished American citizen, and his name is Archie. He's over there in the back row, modestly. I remember that evening, we went around the board, and we got to Archie. Everybody knows his illustrious father and that great public servant. He said, "Bill, nobody has a right or a duty or a responsibility to advise you on such a highly personal matter. This is a matter for your conscience. But my dad was a guy who had some ego, and he was sensible of the need for its restraint. So he always made it a rule that never, under any consideration would he take a public honor for public service."

So I just dropped this into the hopper. The balance was tipped and the enlargement of our Tradition of anonymity, this spiritual foundation of all our Traditions, to include public honors was confirmed.

19 So as best I could, and with some wonder how this great university would receive it when a drunken stockbroker turned them down, I did write this letter, and I'd like to read it to you so as to get it into the record. I thought of leaving it into the files, but maybe this is a good time to share it with you:

Dear Mr. Secretary,

This is my wish to express my deepest thanks to members of the corporation of your great and respected university for considering me as one suitable for the degree of Doctor of Laws. It is only after a most careful consultation with friends and with my conscience that I now feel obliged to decline such a mark of distinction. Were I to accept, the near-term benefit to Alcoholics Anonymous and to those legions that still suffer our malady, would no doubt be worldwide and considerable. I am sure that such a potent endorsement would greatly hasten public approval of AA everywhere.

Therefore, none but the most compelling of reasons could prompt my decision to deny Alcoholics Anonymous an opportunity of this dimension. Now this is the reason: the Tradition of Alcoholics Anonymous, our only means of self-government, entreats each member to avoid all of that particular kind of personal publicity or distinction, which might link his name with our society in the general public's mind.

I think that we AAs are fortunate to be acutely aware that such forces must never be ruling among us, lest we perish altogether. The Tradition of personal anonymity and no honors at the public level is our protective shield. We dare not meet the power of temptation naked. Of course, we quite understand the high value of honors outside of our Fellowship. We always find inspiration when these are deservedly bestowed and humbly received as the hall-marks of distinguished attainment of service.

We only say that in our special circumstances it would be imprudent for us to accept them for AA achievements. For example, my own life story gathered for years around an implacable pursuit of money, fame, and power; this anticlimaxed, by my near-sinking in the sea of alcohol. Though I did survive that grim misadventure, I well understand that the dreaded neurotic germ of the power contagions has survived in me also. It is only dormant, and it can again multiply and rend me and Alcoholics Anonymous too. Tens of thousands of my fellow AAs are temperamentally just like me. Fortunately, they know it and I know it. Hence our Tradition of Anonymity, and hence my clear obligation to decline this single honor with all of the immediate satisfaction and benefit that it could have yielded.

Gratefully yours,

Bill Wilson[3]

The continued practice of the AA principles contained within the Steps and the Traditions of the program allows each member of AA to make spiritual progress without feeling compelled to achieve the impossible goal of spiritual perfection. The understanding and application of anonymity as the spiritual foundation of AA's Traditions will keep the fellowship united. It has often been said by AA members, "I got drunk, *we* get sober." This simple statement illustrates the significance of unity and brings us full circle back to the First Tradition: The common welfare comes first — personal recovery depends upon it. Unity is essential for the survival of the AA fellowship. And this can only be accomplished by placing principles before personalities.

The Need for the Traditions Today and Tomorrow

Members of Alcoholics Anonymous often comment in amazement upon the fact that Bill W. drafted the Twelve Steps and wrote the AA Big Book when there were fewer than one hundred members. Bill himself had just three years of continued sobriety when he began writing the book *Alcoholics Anonymous.* AA members almost uniformly claim that God wrote the Big Book, he just used Bill W. to communicate His message. It would be difficult to debate such a claim when looking at the record.

Since its debut in April of 1939, as of this writing, the Big Book has sold more than thirty million copies and Alcoholics Anonymous has truly become a worldwide fellowship. AA members can take great pride and satisfaction in the fact that AA works today exactly as it did in 1935 — with one alcoholic carrying the message to the next.

In 1945–46, when the Traditions were first being written and introduced to the fellowship, there was concern that somehow AA needed to be protected, mostly from itself. The pioneers knew very well that if AA were ever to collapse it would be from within. It's important to note that membership totals at that time were approaching fifteen thousand with fewer than seven hundred groups. Could Bill W. and his friends have envisioned that AA would one day consist of more than two million members in more than 180 countries, with more than 115,000 registered groups spread throughout the world?

If you ask an old-timer why AA continues to work, you're certain to hear "the Traditions." The Twelve Traditions are the glue that keeps it all together and keeps AA functioning relatively smoothly in this ever-changing world.

I have randomly asked dozens of active AA members the following question: "How much time do you think the average AA member spends per year learning, reading, discussing, or studying the AA Traditions?" Most people questioned suggest that the number of hours spent by the average member on Traditions study is less than ten hours per year. These results are frightening if you believe that these Traditions are the glue that keeps the fellowship together! Should AA be concerned? We know that when the Traditions were first introduced, only a limited number of the membership had any interest at all. Groups that invited Bill to speak asked him to talk about his story and not the Traditions. So, perhaps this seeming apathy toward the Traditions isn't anything new at all. When looking over conference-approved literature for 2011, there seems to be a void when it comes to material on the Traditions. Other than the book *Twelve Steps and Twelve Traditions* (1953) and a couple of pamphlets, there is simply no material available for study.

With this being the case, it raises the question "Is there limited literature because of limited interest, or is there limited interest because there's not enough current or new literature?" Regardless of whether the chicken came before the egg, there appears to be a potential problem developing within AA.

If you were to ask members today if they think there are problems or the potential for problems within AA, you would be almost certain to get an earful. Fears include those about other drug addictions, social media, and court-referred attendees, and some of the older members' concerns are related to the lack of Twelve Step calls. What you probably *won't* hear is that most AA members couldn't recite three of the Twelve Traditions from memory.

Does all this matter? The principles of Alcoholics Anonymous have been practiced for more than seventy-six years, and the organization seems to be just fine. Is this apathy a growing tumor among AA members that will spread and eventually be the demise of the entire movement?

When introducing the "Third Legacy" to the conference of delegates meeting in St. Louis before AA's twentieth anniversary in late June of 1955, Bill W. presented them with a draft copy of the manual entitled *The Third*

Legacy Manual of World Service as Proposed By Bill. Within the manual he shared history of AA and the Traditions.

After discussing the initial response of the membership toward the Traditions, he wrote the following:

> *Only five years later, several thousand AA members, meeting at the 1950 Cleveland Convention, declared that AA's Traditions, by then stated in the now-familiar short form, constituted the platform upon which our Fellowship could best function and hold together in unity for all time to come. They saw that the Twelve Traditions were going to be as necessary to the life of our society as the Twelve Steps were to the life of each member. The AA Traditions were, the Cleveland Convention thought, the key to the unity, the function, and even the survival of us all.* [1]

Throughout the writing of this book, we have attempted to give examples of the importance of the Traditions and how they can be used by individual members and the groups. This book is not intended to be any sort of textbook; we chose to share many experiences members have had with the Traditions and the talks given by Bill and other AA leaders rather than doing a scholarly thesis. Much more could also be written on the practical application of the Traditions as a guide or workbook.

Back in the mid-1980s, Joe and Charlie began doing seminars "To Bring the Big Book Alive." Some AA members scoffed at this idea, stating that they didn't need anyone's help or suggestions regarding the study of the Big Book. Nevertheless, tens of thousands of members attended these workshops over a period of twenty-five years. Many dedicated AA members claim that by attending one of these workshops, their excitement for both the Big Book and the program was ignited.

Today in most cities throughout the United States, there are various workshops on the Twelve Steps being conducted by members. Again, for some members there seems to be great value in attending these workshops and studying in a group setting. Perhaps if sponsors introduced the Traditions to their sponsees and groups hosted workshops, members could share their experience with the Traditions, and it would catch on like the Big Book study workshops.

Like anything else in AA, these things happen slowly, but in some areas this type of thing has already begun. Hopefully, the idea of communicating the importance of the Traditions in informal yet meaningful ways will encourage others to do the same. The Traditions should not be used as a club with which to beat someone down; they should be used as principles to help lift up people. Can unity, humility, love, and unselfishness be transmitted to all who enter through the threshold of AA? Is this not what the Traditions teach?

Most AA members recognize their personal responsibility to carry the message to the next suffering alcoholic. Perhaps included in this message should be the value of the Traditions. It is often said, "Don't tell me what you do — it's your example that makes it clear." The example passed on by those who live by the AA

Traditions will speak louder and more effectively than words can ever do. The principles contained within them will keep Alcoholics Anonymous united and protected forever. The following poem has been a favorite of AA members for years:

Sermons We See

I'd rather see a sermon than hear one any day.
I'd rather one would walk with me than merely show
the way,
The eye is a better pupil and more willing than the ear.
Fine counsel is confusing but examples always clear.
The best of all the preachers are the ones who live
their creeds.
For to see good put into action is what everyone needs.
I soon can learn to do it if you let me see it done.
I can watch your hands in action, but your tongue too
fast may run.
The lectures you deliver may be very wise and true.
But I would rather get my lessons by observing what
you do.
I may not understand the high advice that you may give.
But there is no misunderstanding how you act and how
you live.[2]

Bill W.'s April 1946 A.A. *Grapevine* Article "Twelve Suggested Points for A.A. Tradition"

Nobody invented Alcoholics Anonymous. It grew.
Trial and error has produced a rich experience. Little by
little we have been adopting the lessons of that experience, first as policy and then as tradition. That process
still goes on and we hope it never stops. Should we ever
harden too much the letter might crush the spirit. We
could victimize ourselves by petty rules and prohibi-
tions; we could imagine that we had said the last word.
We might even be asking alcoholics to accept our rigid
ideas or stay away. May we never stifle progress like that!

Yet the lessons of our experience count for a great
deal — a very great deal, we are each convinced. The
first written record of A.A. experience was the book,
Alcoholics Anonymous. It was addressed to the heart of
our foremost problem — release from the alcohol obsession. It contained personal experiences of drinking and
recovery and a statement of those divine but ancient
principles which have brought us a miraculous regen-

eration. Since publication of *Alcoholics Anonymous* in 1939 we have grown from 100 to 24,000 members. Seven years have passed; seven years of vast experience with our next greatest undertaking — the problem of living and working together. This is today our main concern. If we can succeed in this adventure — and keep succeeding — then, and only then, will our future be secure.

Since personal calamity holds us in bondage no more, our most challenging concern has become the future of Alcoholics Anonymous; how to preserve among us A.A.s such a powerful unity that neither weakness of persons nor the strain and strife of these troubled times can harm our common cause. We know that *Alcoholics Anonymous* must continue to live. Else, save few exceptions, we and our brother alcoholics throughout the world will surely resume the hopeless journey to oblivion.

Almost any A.A. can tell you what our group problems are. Fundamentally they have to do with our relations, one with the other, and with the world outside. They involve relations of the A.A. to his group, the relation of his group to Alcoholics Anonymous as a whole, and the place of Alcoholics Anonymous in that troubled sea called Modern Society, where all of humankind must presently shipwreck or find haven. Terribly relevant is the problem of our basic structure and our attitude toward those ever pressing questions of leadership, money and authority. The future may well depend on how we feel and act about things that are controversial and how we regard our public relations. Our final destiny will surely hang upon what we presently decide to do with these danger-fraught issues!

Now comes the crux of our discussion. It is this: Have we yet acquired sufficient experience to state clear-cut policies on these, our chief concerns? Can we now declare general principles which could grow into vital traditions — traditions sustained in the heart of each A.A. by his own deep conviction and by the common consent of his fellows? That is the question. Though full answer to all our perplexities may never be found, I'm sure we have come at last to a vantage point whence we can discern the main outlines of a body of tradition; which, God willing, can stand as an effective guard against all the ravages of time and circumstance.

Acting upon the persistent urge of old A.A. friends, and upon the conviction that general agreement and consent between our members is now possible, I shall venture to place in words these suggestions for *An Alcoholics Anonymous Tradition of Relations — Twelve Points to Assure Our Future:*

Our A.A. Experience Has Taught Us That:

1. — Each member of Alcoholics Anonymous *is* but a small part of a great whole. A.A. must continue to live or most of us will surely die. Hence our common welfare comes first. But individual welfare follows close afterward.

2. — For our Group purpose there is but one ultimate authority — a loving God as He may express Himself in our Group conscience.

3. — Our membership ought to include all who suffer alcoholism. Hence we may refuse none who wish to recover. Nor ought A.A. membership ever depend upon money or conformity. Any two or three alcoholics gathered together for sobriety may call themselves an A.A. Group.

4. — With respect to its own affairs, each A.A. Group should be responsible to no other authority than its own conscience. But when its plans concern the welfare of neighboring groups also, those groups ought to be consulted. And no group, regional committee or individual should ever take any action that might greatly affect A.A. as a whole without conferring with the Trustees of The Alcoholic Foundation. On such issues our common welfare is paramount.

5. — Each Alcoholics Anonymous Group ought to be a spiritual entity *having but one primary purpose* — that of carrying its message to the alcoholic who still suffers.

6. — Problems of money, property and authority may easily divert us from our primary spiritual aim. We think, therefore, that any considerable property of genuine use to A.A. should be separately incorporated and managed, thus dividing the material from the spiritual. An A.A. Group, as such, should never go into business. Secondary aids to A.A., such as clubs or hospitals which require much property or administration, ought to be so set apart, that if necessary, they can be freely discarded by the Groups. The

Bill W.'s April 1946 A.A. *Grapevine* Article

management of these special facilities should be the sole responsibility of those people, whether A.A.s or not, who financially support them. For our clubs, we prefer A.A. managers. But hospitals, as well as other places of recuperation, ought to be well outside A.A. — and medically supervised. An A.A. Group may cooperate with anyone, but should bind itself to no one.

7. — The A.A. Groups themselves ought to be fully supported by the voluntary contributions of their own members. We think that each Group should soon achieve this ideal; that any public solicitation of funds using the name of Alcoholics Anonymous is highly dangerous; that acceptance of large gifts from any source or of contributions carrying any obligation whatever, is usually unwise. Then, too, we view with much concern those A.A. treasuries which continue, beyond prudent reserves, to accumulate funds for no stated A.A. purpose. Experience has often warned us that nothing can so surely destroy our spiritual heritage as futile disputes over property, money, and authority.

8. — Alcoholics Anonymous should remain forever non-professional. We define professionalism as the occupation of counseling alcoholics for fees or hire. But we may employ alcoholics where they are going to perform those full time services for which we might otherwise have to engage non-alcoholics. Such special services may be well recompensed. But personal "12th Step" work is never to be paid for.

9. — Each A.A. Group needs the least possible organization. Rotating leadership is usually the best. The small group may elect its secretary, the large group its rotating committee, and the groups of a large metropolitan area their central committee, which often employs a full time secretary. The trustees of The Alcoholic Foundation are, in effect, our General Service Committee. They are the custodians of our A.A. tradition and the receivers of voluntary A.A. contributions by which they maintain A.A. General Headquarters and our General Secretary at New York. They are authorized by the groups to handle our overall public relations and they guarantee the integrity of our principal publication, *The A.A. Grapevine.* All such representatives are to be guided in the spirit of service, for true leaders in A.A. are but trusted and experienced servants of the whole. They derive no real authority from their titles. Universal respect is the key to their usefulness.

10. — No A.A. group or member should ever, *in such a way as to implicate A.A.,* express any opinion on outside controversial issues — particularly those of politics, alcohol reform or sectarian religion. The Alcoholics Anonymous groups oppose no one. Concerning such matters they can express no views whatever.

11. — Our relations with the outside world should be characterized by modesty and anonymity. We think A.A. ought to avoid sensational advertising. Our public relations should be guided by the principle of attraction rather than promotion. There is never need to praise ourselves. We feel it better to let our friends recommend us.

12.   — And finally, we of Alcoholics Anonymous believe that the principle of anonymity has an immense spiritual significance. It reminds us that we are to place principles before personalities; that we are actually to practice a truly humble modesty. This to the end that our great blessings may never spoil us; that we shall forever live in thankful contemplation of Him who presides over us all.

May it be urged that while these principles have been stated in rather positive language they are still only suggestions for our future. We of Alcoholics Anonymous have never enthusiastically responded to any assumption of personal authority. Perhaps it is well for A.A., that this is true. So I offer these suggestions neither as one man's dictum nor as a creed of any kind, but rather as a first attempt to portray that group ideal toward which we have assuredly been led by a Higher Power these ten years past.

P.S. To help free discussion I would like to amplify the *Twelve Points of Tradition* in future *Grapvine* pieces.

The article entitled "Twelve Suggested Points for A.A. Tradition" is reprinted with permission of the A.A. Grapevine, Inc.

Appendix B

The Twelve Traditions of Alcoholics Anonymous
(Short Form)

One — Our common welfare should come first; personal recovery depends upon A.A. unity.

Two — For our group purpose there is but one ultimate authority — a loving God as He may express Himself in our group conscience. Our leaders are but trusted servants; they do not govern.

Three — The only requirement for A.A. membership is a desire to stop drinking.

Four — Each group should be autonomous except in matters affecting other groups or A.A. as a whole.

Five — Each group has but one primary purpose — to carry its message to the alcoholic who still suffers.

Six — An A.A. group ought never endorse, finance, or lend the A.A. name to any related facility or outside enterprise, lest problems of money, property and prestige divert us from our primary purpose.

Seven — Every A.A. group ought to be fully self-supporting, declining outside contributions.

Eight — Alcoholics Anonymous should remain forever nonprofessional, but our service centers may employ special workers.

Nine — A.A., as such, ought never be organized; but we may create service boards or committees directly responsible to those they serve.

Ten — Alcoholics Anonymous has no opinion on outside issues; hence the A.A. name ought never be drawn into public controversy.

Eleven — Our public relations policy is based on attraction rather than promotion; we need always maintain personal anonymity at the level of press, radio and films.

Twelve — Anonymity is the spiritual foundation of all our Traditions, ever reminding us to place principles before personalities.

Reprinted from *Alcoholics Anonymous,* 4th ed. (New York: Alcoholics Anonymous World Services, 2001), 562.

Appendix C

The Twelve Traditions of Alcoholics Anonymous

(Long Form)

Our A.A. experience has taught us that:

One — Each member of Alcoholics Anonymous is but a small part of a great whole. A.A. must continue to live or most of us will surely die. Hence our common welfare comes first. But individual welfare follows close afterward.

Two — For our group purpose there is but one ultimate authority — a loving God as He may express Himself in our group conscience.

Three — Our membership ought to include all who suffer from alcoholism. Hence we may refuse none who wish to recover. Nor ought A.A. membership ever depend upon money or conformity. Any two or three alcoholics gathered together for sobriety may call themselves an A.A. group, provided that, as a group, they have no other affiliation.

Four — With respect to its own affairs, each A.A. group should be responsible to no other authority than its own conscience. But when its plans concern the welfare of neighboring groups also, those groups ought to be consulted. And no group, regional committee, or individual should ever take any action that might greatly affect A.A. as a whole without conferring with the trustees of the General Service Board. On such issues our common welfare is paramount.

Five — Each Alcoholics Anonymous group ought to be a spiritual entity *having but one primary purpose* — that of carrying its message to the alcoholic who still suffers.

Six — Problems of money, property, and authority may easily divert us from our primary spiritual aim. We think, therefore, that any considerable property of genuine use to A.A. should be separately incorporated and managed, thus dividing the material from the spiritual. An A.A. group, as such, should never go into business. Secondary aids to A.A., such as clubs or hospitals which require much property or administration, ought to be incorporated and so set apart that, if necessary, they can be freely discarded by the groups. Hence such facilities ought not to use the A.A. name. Their management should be the sole responsibility of those people who financially support them. For clubs, A.A. managers are usually preferred. But hospitals, as well as other places of recuperation, ought to be well outside A.A. — and medically supervised. While an A.A. group may cooperate with anyone, such cooperation ought never to go so far as affiliation or endorsement, actual or implied. An A.A. group can bind itself to no one.

Seven — The A.A. groups themselves ought to be fully supported by the voluntary contributions of their own members. We think that each group should soon achieve this ideal; that any public solicitation of funds using the name of Alcoholics Anonymous is highly dangerous, whether by groups, clubs, hospitals, or other outside agencies; that acceptance of large gifts from any source, or of contributions carrying any obligation whatever, is unwise. Then too, we view with much concern those A.A. treasuries which continue, beyond prudent reserves, to accumulate funds for no stated A.A. purpose. Experience has often warned us that nothing can so surely destroy our spiritual heritage as futile disputes over property, money, and authority.

Eight — Alcoholics Anonymous should remain forever nonprofessional. We define professionalism as the occupation of counseling alcoholics for fees or hire. But we may employ alcoholics where they are going to perform those services for which we may otherwise have to engage nonalcoholics. Such special services may be well recompensed. But our usual A.A. Twelfth Step work is never to be paid for.

Nine — Each A.A. group needs the least possible organization. Rotating leadership is the best.

The small group may elect its secretary, the large group its rotating committee, and the groups of a large metropolitan area their central or intergroup committee, which often employs a full-time secretary. The trustees of the General Service Board are, in effect, our A.A. General Service Committee. They are the custodians of our A.A. Tradition and the receivers of voluntary A.A. contributions by which we maintain our A.A. General Service Office at New York. They are authorized by the groups to handle our overall public relations and they guarantee the integrity of our principal newspaper, the *A.A. Grapevine*. All such representatives are to be guided in the spirit of service, for true leaders in A.A. are but trusted and experienced servants of the whole. They derive no real authority from their titles; they do not govern. Universal respect is the key to their usefulness.

Ten — No A.A. group or member should ever, in such a way as to implicate A.A., express any opinion on outside controversial issues — particularly those of politics, alcohol reform, or sectarian religion. The Alcoholics Anonymous groups oppose no one. Concerning such matters they can express no views whatever.

Eleven — Our relations with the general public should be characterized by personal anonymity.

We think A.A. ought to avoid sensational advertising. Our names and pictures as A.A. members ought not be broadcast, filmed, or publicly printed. Our public relations should be guided by the principle of attraction rather than promotion. There is never need to praise ourselves. We feel it better to let our friends recommend us.

Twelve — And finally, we of Alcoholics Anonymous believe that the principle of anonymity has an immense spiritual significance. It reminds us that we are to place principles before personalities; that we are actually to practice a genuine humility. This to the end that our great blessings may never spoil us; that we shall forever live in thankful contemplation of Him who presides over us all.

Appendix D

The Twelve Steps of Alcoholics Anonymous

1. We admitted we were powerless over alcohol — that our lives had become unmanageable.

2. Came to believe that a Power greater than ourselves could restore us to sanity.

3. Made a decision to turn our will and our lives over to the care of God *as we understood Him.*

4. Made a searching and fearless moral inventory of ourselves.

5. Admitted to God, to ourselves, and to another human being the exact nature of our wrongs.

6. Were entirely ready to have God remove all these defects of character.

7. Humbly asked Him to remove our shortcomings.

8. Made a list of all persons we had harmed, and became willing to make amends to them all.

9. Made direct amends to such people wherever possible, except when to do so would injure them or others.

10. Continued to take personal inventory and when we were wrong promptly admitted it.

11. Sought through prayer and meditation to improve our conscious contact with God, *as we understood Him,* praying only for knowledge of His will for us and the power to carry that out.

12. Having had a spiritual awakening as the result of these Steps, we tried to carry this message to alcoholics, and to practice these principles in all our affairs.

Notes

Introduction

1. Nell Wing, *Grateful to Have Been There: My 42 Years with Bill and Lois, and the Evolution of Alcoholics Anonymous* (Park Ridge, IL: Parkside Publishing, 1992), 20.

2. "Quote DB," www.quotedb.com/quotes/3280.

3. *Alcoholics Anonymous,* 4th ed. (New York: Alcoholics Anonymous World Services, 2001), 30.

4. Ibid., xiii.

5. Ibid., "Foreword to First Edition," xiii–xiv.

6. "Tradition One," in *Twelve Steps and Twelve Traditions* (New York: Alcoholics Anonymous World Services, 1981), 129.

Chapter 1: Our Common Welfare

1. Bill W., speech, First International Convention of AA, Cleveland, OH, July 28–30, 1950, transcribed by Michael Fitzpatrick. Fitzpatrick Archive, www.recoveryspeakers.org.

2. Ollie L., speech, First International Convention of AA, Cleveland, OH, July 28–30, 1950, transcribed by Michael Fitzpatrick. Fitzpatrick Archive, www.recoveryspeakers.org.

3. *Alcoholics Anonymous,* 4th ed. (New York: Alcoholics Anonymous World Services, 2001), 162.

4. "Tradition One," in *Twelve Steps and Twelve Traditions* (New York: Alcoholics Anonymous World Services, 1981), 129.

5. Bill W., speech, Third International Convention of AA, Long Beach, CA, July 2–4, 1960.

Chapter 2: One Ultimate Authority

1. "Tradition Two," in *Twelve Steps and Twelve Traditions* (New York: Alcoholics Anonymous World Services, 1981), 132, 189.

2. Bill W., speech, Chicago, IL, February 1951, transcribed by Michael Fitzpatrick. Fitzpatrick Archive, www.recoveryspeakers.org.

3. Los Angeles Group letter, copy in Fitzpatrick Archive.

4. *Alcoholics Anonymous Comes of Age* (New York: Alcoholics Anonymous World Services, 1957), 99.

5. Ollie L., speech, First International Convention of AA, Cleveland, OH, July 28–30, 1950, transcribed by Michael Fitzpatrick. Fitzpatrick Archive, www.recoveryspeakers.org.

6. Howard P., interview with Michael Fitzpatrick, Gilbert, AZ, June 2011.

Chapter 3: No Barriers to Entry

1. *Alcoholics Anonymous,* 4th ed. (New York: Alcoholics Anonymous World Services, 2001), 17.

2. Bill W., speech, Memphis, TN, 1947, transcribed by Michael Fitzpatrick. Fitzpatrick Archive, www.recoveryspeakers.org.

3. Barry L., speech, Michigan, 1985, transcribed by Michael Fitzpatrick. Fitzpatrick Archive, www.recoveryspeakers.org.

4. Ibid.

5. *Twelve Steps and Twelve Traditions* (New York: Alcoholics Anonymous World Services, 1981), 140–41.

6. Dick S., speech, First International Convention of AA, Cleveland, OH, July 1950, transcribed by Michael Fitzpatrick. Fitzpatrick Archive, www.recoveryspeakers.org.

7. Bill W., speech, Chicago, IL, February 1951, transcribed by Michael Fitzpatrick. Fitzpatrick Archive, www.recoveryspeakers.org.

8. Bill W., speech, Third International Convention of AA, Long Beach, CA, July 1960, transcribed by Michael Fitzpatrick. Fitzpatrick Archive, www.recoveryspeakers.org.

Chapter 4: Group Autonomy

1. "Tradition One," in *Twelve Steps and Twelve Traditions* (New York: Alcoholics Anonymous World Services, 1981), 129.

2. *Alcoholics Anonymous Comes of Age* (New York: Alcoholics Anonymous World Services, 1957), 103.

3. "The Twelve Traditions (The Long Form): Tradition Four," in *Twelve Steps and Twelve Traditions* (New York: Alcoholics Anonymous World Services, 1981), 189.

4. Arthur H. Cain, "Alcoholics Can Be Cured—Despite A.A.," *Saturday Evening Post,* September 19, 1964.

5. Marc Fisher, "Seeking Recovery, Finding Confusion," *Washington Post,* July 22, 2007, www.washingtonpost.com/wp-dyn/content/article/2007/07/21/AR2007072101356.html.

6. "Tradition Three," in *Twelve Steps and Twelve Traditions* (New York: Alcoholics Anonymous World Services, 1981), 139.

7. Barry L., speech, Michigan, 1985, transcribed by Michael Fitzpatrick. Fitzpatrick Archive, www.recoveryspeakers.org.

8. *Alcoholics Anonymous,* 4th ed. (New York: Alcoholics Anonymous World Services, 2001), 44.

9. Dick S., speech, First International Convention of AA, Cleveland, OH, July 1950, transcribed by Michael Fitzpatrick. Fitzpatrick Archive, www.recoveryspeakers.org.

10. Bill W., "Editorial: On the 4th Tradition," *A. A. Grapevine* IV, no. 10 (March 1948): 2.

Chapter 5: Why the Shoemaker Should Stick to His Last

1. "Tradition Five," in *Twelve Steps and Twelve Traditions* (New York: Alcoholics Anonymous World Services, 1981), 150.

2. Ibid.

3. Ibid.

4. Nell Wing, *Grateful to Have Been There: My 42 Years with Bill and Lois, and the Evolution of Alcoholics Anonymous* (Park Ridge, IL: Parkside Publishing, 1992), 28.

5. Ibid.

6. Bill W.'s speech at Texas State Convention in Ft. Worth, June 13, 1954, transcribed by Michael Fitzpatrick. Fitzpatrick Archive, www.recoveryspeakers.org.

7. Ibid.

8. Gene from Toledo, speech at First International Convention of AA, Cleveland, OH, July 1950, transcribed by Michael Fitzpatrick. Fitzpatrick Archive, www.recoveryspeakers.org.

9. Michael Fitzpatrick's conversation with anonymous alcoholic, Phoenix, AZ, February 2010.

10. *Twelve Steps and Twelve Traditions* (New York: Alcoholics Anonymous World Services, 1981), 150.

11. Michael Fitzpatrick's conversation with anonymous alcoholic, Phoenix, AZ, February 2010.

Chapter 6: Stability through Sacrifice

1. *Alcoholics Anonymous,* 2nd ed. (New York: Alcoholics Anonymous Publishing, 1955); *Twelve Steps and Twelve Traditions* (New York: Alcoholics Anonymous World Services, 1981), 190.

2. Ibid., 564.

3. Nell Wing, *Grateful to Have Been There: My 42 Years with Bill and Lois, and the Evolution of Alcoholics Anonymous* (Park Ridge, IL: Parkside Publishing, 1992), 12.

4. Bill W., speech, Third International Convention of AA, Long Beach, CA, July 1960, transcribed by Michael Fitzpatrick. Fitzpatrick Archive, www.recoveryspeakers.org.

5. Tom I., phone interview with Michael Fitzpatrick, June 20, 2011.

6. Gene from Toledo, speech at First International Convention of AA, Cleveland, OH, July 1950, transcribed by Michael Fitzpatrick. Fitzpatrick Archive, www.recoveryspeakers.org.

Chapter 7: Paying Our Own Way

1. "Tradition Seven," in *Twelve Steps and Twelve Traditions* (New York: Alcoholics Anonymous World Services, 1981), 160.

2. Howard P., interview with Michael Fitzpatrick, Gilbert, AZ, June 11, 2011.

3. Fred from Florida, speech at First International Convention of AA, Cleveland, OH, July 1950, transcribed by Michael Fitzpatrick. Fitzpatrick Archive, www.recoveryspeakers.org.

4. Michael Fitzpatrick's conversation with anonymous AA member, Phoenix, AZ, February 2010.

Chapter 8: Freely Ye Have Received, Freely Give

1. "Tradition Eight," in *Twelve Steps and Twelve Traditions* (New York: Alcoholics Anonymous World Services, 1981), 166.

2. Ibid.

3. Speech at First International Convention of AA, Cleveland, OH, July 1950, transcribed by Michael Fitzpatrick. Fitzpatrick Archive, www.recoveryspeakers.org.

4. Tom I., phone interview with Michael Fitzpatrick, June 20, 2011.

Chapter 9: An Anarchy That Works

1. "Tradition Nine," in *Twelve Steps and Twelve Traditions* (New York: Alcoholics Anonymous World Services, 1981), 172.

2. *Alcoholics Anonymous*, 4th ed. (New York: Alcoholics Anonymous World Services, 2001), 1.

3. George from Carlsbad, speech at First International Convention of AA, Cleveland, OH, July 1950, transcribed by Michael Fitzpatrick. Fitzpatrick Archive, www.recoveryspeakers.org.

4. "The Twelve Traditions (The Long Form): Tradition Nine," in *Twelve Steps and Twelve Traditions* (New York: Alcoholics Anonymous World Services, 1981), 191–92.

5. See appendix A for this article.

6. *Pass It On: The Story of Bill Wilson and How the A.A. Message Reached the World* (New York: Alcoholics Anonymous World Services, 1984), 373.

7. Dr. Bob S., farewell speech, First International Convention of AA, Cleveland, OH, July 1950, transcribed by Michael Fitzpatrick. Fitzpatrick Archive, www.recoveryspeakers.org.

Chapter 10: Staying Out of the Fray

1. George from Carlsbad, First International Convention of AA, Cleveland, OH, July 1950, transcribed by Michael Fitzpatrick. Fitzpatrick Archive, www.recoveryspeakers.org.

2. Nell Wing, *Grateful to Have Been There: My 42 Years with Bill and Lois, and the Evolution of Alcoholics Anonymous* (Park Ridge, IL: Parkside Publishing, 1992).

3. Bill W., "Twelve Concepts for World Service" in *The A.A. Service Manual Combined With Twelve Concepts for World Service*, 2011–2012 ed. (New York: Alcoholics Anonymous World Services, 2011), 68. Available at www.aa.org/catalog.cfm?category=8&product=100.

4. "Estimates of A.A. Groups and Members," Alcoholics Anonymous, www.aa.org/subpage.cfm?page=74.

5. Bill W., speech, First International Convention of AA, Cleveland, OH, 1950, transcribed by Michael Fitzpatrick. Fitzpatrick Archive, www.recoveryspeakers.org.

6. *Twelve Steps and Twelve Traditions* (New York: Alcoholics Anonymous World Services, 1981), 98.

Chapter 11: Anonymity: A Key to AA's Survival

1. Bill W., farewell message, October 1970, copied from a photograph of the framed message found at Stepping Stones, The Historic Home of Bill and Lois Wilson, Bedford Hills, NY.

2. "Tradition Eleven," in *Twelve Steps and Twelve Traditions* (New York: Alcoholics Anonymous World Services, 1981), 180.

3. Conversation with anonymous member, Phoenix, AZ, February 2010.

4. "Challenging the Second 'A' in AA," *New York Times*, May 6, 2011, page ST1.

5. Ibid.

6. Kylie from Boston, speech at First International Convention of AA, Cleveland, OH, July 1950, transcribed by Michael Fitzpatrick. Fitzpatrick Archive, www.recoveryspeakers.org.

7. Bill W., speech, First International Convention of AA, Cleveland, OH, July 1950, transcribed by Michael Fitzpatrick. Fitzpatrick Archive, www.recoveryspeakers.org.

Chapter 12: Principles Before Personalities

1. Video interview with Abraham Hoffer, Community Addiction Recovery Association, 2007, www.youtube.com/watch?v=PH1_v0zh_gk.

2. "Tradition Twelve," in *Twelve Steps and Twelve Traditions* (New York: Alcoholics Anonymous World Services, 1981), 184.

3. Bill W., speech, Long Beach, CA, 1960, transcribed by Michael Fitzpatrick. Fitzpatrick Archive, www.recoveryspeakers.org.

Epilogue: The Need for the Traditions Today and Tomorrow

1. Draft document by Alcoholics Anonymous, "The Third Legacy Manual of World Service proposed by Bill" (New York: Alcoholics Anonymous General Service Headquarters, June 1955).

2. Edgar A. Guest, "Sermons We See," in *The Light of Faith*, 1st ed. (Chicago: The Reilly and Lee Co., 1926), 163.

About the Authors

Mel B., a resident of Toledo, Ohio, since 1972, is a writer specializing in recovery, timely business topics, speeches, publicity, and military history. Retired since 1986, he served in public relations for a major corporation headquartered in Toledo.

Mel B. is a recovering alcoholic and a longtime member of Alcoholics Anonymous. He writes anonymously on subjects related to alcoholism and was a contributing writer for *Pass It On,* AA's authorized biography of cofounder Bill Wilson. In addition to *Ebby: The Man Who Sponsored Bill W.,* he has authored four other Hazelden books: *New Wine, My Search for Bill W., Walk in Dry Places,* and *101 Meeting Starters,* as well as several Hazelden pamphlets. He has also contributed about sixty articles to *The Grapevine,* the international journal of AA.

Michael Fitzpatrick is coauthor with William G. Borchert of *1000 Years of Sobriety* and is one of the leading historians and speakers in the field of alcoholism, specializing in the development of the Twelve Step movement. He owns what is possibly the largest audio archive related to the Twelve Step movement ever assembled, containing more than three thousand original reel-to-reel recordings of the voices of the men and women who pioneered the Twelve Step movement. Mike is in the process of digitizing these recordings, which are now being made available online at recoveryspeakers.org. Many of the transcripts in this book and recordings included in the accompanying CD and e-book are from this archive.

Mike lives in Chandler, Arizona, with his wife, Joy, and their three children. He and Joy work together to operate his business as a book broker and marketing consultant. Over the years Mike has written sales promotional pieces and training manuals for several major corporations.

He has traveled extensively throughout the United States and Canada as a guest speaker and sales leader, motivating and inspiring his audiences with both his humor and his inspirational message of hope. His message to sales organizations is "attitude is everything!"

Hazelden, a national nonprofit organization founded in 1949, helps people reclaim their lives from the disease of addiction. Built on decades of knowledge and experience, Hazelden offers a comprehensive approach to addiction that addresses the full range of patient, family, and professional needs, including treatment and continuing care for youth and adults, research, higher learning, public education and advocacy, and publishing.

A life of recovery is lived "one day at a time." Hazelden publications, both educational and inspirational, support and strengthen lifelong recovery. In 1954, Hazelden published *Twenty-Four Hours a Day*, the first daily meditation book for recovering alcoholics, and Hazelden continues to publish works to inspire and guide individuals in treatment and recovery, and their loved ones. Professionals who work to prevent and treat addiction also turn to Hazelden for evidence-based curricula, informational materials, and videos for use in schools, treatment programs, and correctional programs.

Through published works, Hazelden extends the reach of hope, encouragement, help, and support to individuals, families, and communities affected by addiction and related issues.

For questions about Hazelden publications, please call **800-328-9000** or visit us online at **hazelden.org/bookstore**.